Tales from the
Heart of the Balkans

World Folklore Advisory Board

Tales from the Heart of the Balkans

Retold by
BONNIE C. MARSHALL

Edited by Vasa D. Mihailovich
Professor Emeritus
University of North Carolina, Chapel Hill

2001
Libraries Unlimited, Inc.
Englewood, Colorado

LIBRARIES UNLIMITED, INC.
P.O. Box 6633
Englewood, CO 80155-6633
1-800-237-6124
www.lu.com

Library of Congress Cataloging-in-Publication Data

Marshall, Bonnie C.
    Tales from the heart of the Balkans / retold by Bonnie C. Marshall ; edited by Vasa D. Mihailovich.
        p. cm. -- (World folklore series)
    Includes bibliographical references and index.
    ISBN 1-56308-870-3 (cloth)
        1. Tales--Balkan Peninsula. 2. Folklore--Balkan Peninsula. I. Mihailovich, Vasa D.
II. Title. III. Series.

GR250 M38 2001
398.2'09496--dc21

                                                                    2001029623

World Folklore Series

Folk Stories of the Hmong: Peoples of Laos, Thailand, and Vietnam. By Norma J. Livo and Dia Cha.

Images of a People: Tlingit Myths and Legends. By Mary Helen Pelton and Jacqueline DiGennaro.

Hyena and the Moon: Stories to Tell from Kenya. By Heather McNeil.

The Corn Woman: Stories and Legends of the Hispanic Southwest. Retold by Angel Vigil.

Thai Tales: Folktales of Thailand. Retold by Supaporn Vathanaprida. Edited by Margaret Read MacDonald.

In Days Gone By: Folklore and Traditions of the Pennsylvania Dutch. By Audrey Burie Kirchner and Margaret R. Tassia.

From the Mango Tree and Other Folktales from Nepal. By Kavita Ram Shrestha and Sarah Lamstein.

Why Ostriches Don't Fly and Other Tales from the African Bush. By I. Murphy Lewis.

The Magic Egg and Other Tales from Ukraine. Retold by Barbara J. Suwyn. Edited by Natalie O. Kononenko.

When Night Falls, Kric! Krac! Haitian Folktales. By Liliane Nerette Louis. Edited by Fred J. Hay.

Jasmine and Coconuts: South Indian Tales. By Cathy Spagnoli and Paramasivam Samanna.

The Enchanted Wood and Other Folktales from Finland. By Norma J. Livo and George O. Livo.

A Tiger by the Tail and Other Stories from the Heart of Korea. Retold by Lindy Soon Curry. Edited by Chan-eung Park.

The Eagle on the Cactus: Traditional Stories from Mexico. Retold by Angel Vigil.

Tales from the Heart of the Balkans. Retold by Bonnie C. Marshall. Edited by Vasa D. Mihailovich.

The Celtic Breeze: Stories of the Otherworld from Scotland, Ireland, and Wales. By Heather McNeil.

Selections Available on Audiocassette

Hyena and the Moon: Stories to Tell from Kenya. By Heather McNeil.

The Corn Woman: Stories and Legends of the Hispanic Southwest. Retold by Angel Vigil.

Thai Tales: Folktales of Thailand. Retold by Supaporn Vathanaprida. Edited by Margaret Read MacDonald.

Folk Stories of the Hmong: Peoples of Laos, Thailand, and Vietnam. By Norma J. Livo and Dia Cha.

Contents

Part I
MYTHS AND LEGENDS

COLORED PHOTOGRAPHS

Part II
ANIMAL TALES

Part III
FAIRY TALES

Part IV
TALES OF EVERYDAY LIFE

Foreword

Vasa D. Mihailovich

The Balkans, both South Slavic and non-Slavic, have been known as a fertile ground for folk songs, folktales, fairy tales, proverbs, and other forms of folklore. For many centuries these literary expressions were preserved and passed from generation to generation orally because literacy was limited to the top layer of the respective societies, while the "folk"—the true source of folklore—were left to their inborn sense of artistic creativity.

Only when a Serb, Vuk Stefanović Karadžić, collected and published Serbian folk songs and tales was the world made aware of this great treasure. Karadžić did his collecting during the period of romanticism (the middle of the nineteenth century) when interest in folk literature was at its peak and had become one of the mainstays of the romantic movement. This made it possible for many leading European writers, such as Johann Wolfgang von Goethe, Sir Walter Scott, Aleksandr Pushkin, Adam Mickiewicz, and others, not only to read and enjoy these gems, but also to aid in their dissemination by giving them their stamps of approval.

The volume at hand illustrates the high quality and immense variety of South Slavic and Balkan folktales. The compiler and translator has collected tales from various ethnic groups living in the countries, and even in specific regions within the countries, that once comprised Yugoslavia. Thus, the volume contains tales from Yugoslavia (Serbia) as well as from Montenegro and Kosovo and Metohija within Yugoslavia; from Croatia as well as from Dalmatia and Istria within Croatia. In addition, there are tales from Albanians and Romanies (Gypsies) of the area.

The reader is treated to a panoply of themes, sometimes showing a slightly different approach to a basic theme. Moreover, the tales reveal many themes present in folktales throughout the world, demonstrating that the Balkans is an inseparable part of the world community. For scholars in the field, there are suggestions of comparative possibilities.

More importantly, general readers will find, I am sure, plenty of fascinating and enjoyable reading in this book. Coming as it does at a crucial moment in history—a time of conflict between the nations of this region—the book will help readers understand the background and historical makeup of this corner of the world so unfortunately beset by war and strife. It will also help them understand that despite all the differences and confrontations, there is a common ground on which this area can be approached. War is transient, but the peoples and their artistic acumen prevail. This book is a powerful testimonial of the universality of human beings everywhere in the world, the Balkans not excepted. Years from now that testimonial will hold even truer.

Preface and Acknowledgments

It has been more than thirty years since the last comprehensive English-language publication of a collection of folktales from the area on the Balkan Peninsula known until recently as Yugoslavia. Teachers, students, librarians, and general readers are without a fresh work and most likely without any work at all representative of the area because out-of-print books are difficult to obtain. The seriousness of this inadequacy of resources is particularly noticeable now that the Balkan countries are the focus of world attention.

This collection of South Slavic and Balkan folktales, along with the introductory material, is meant to provide information on an area about which we understand little. Representative stories from all the countries of the former Yugoslavia are included. Where appropriate, stories from prominent regions within specific countries are featured. It is my hope that in addition to acquiring knowledge, the reader will enjoy a folkloric journey through Yugoslavia (Serbia and Montenegro), Macedonia, Bosnia and Herzegovina, Croatia, and Slovenia.

Collecting, translating, and adapting (or retelling) folktales from the Serbian, Croatian, Macedonian, and Slovenian languages was a fascinating labor of love for me. Initially, I read through everything existent in English, after which I made translations of stories that had never before been rendered in English, so that the collection would be a new contribution and not a repetition of what had already been done. It is my sincere hope that readers enjoy reading or hearing the stories as much as I enjoyed translating them. (Further notes on translation and languages follow notes on the oral literature.)

The preparation of this collection would have been impossible without the help and moral support of the editor, Professor Emeritus Vasa D. Mihailovich of the University of North Carolina. It was he who introduced me to Yugoslav literature and who constantly provided inspiration and guidance. A very special thanks goes to him for his advice, the loan and gift of materials, and for his invaluable assistance with the initial translations.

I am grateful to the library staffs at Davis Library of the University of North Carolina at Chapel Hill, the E. H. Little Library of Davidson College, and Meredith Public Library in Meredith, New Hampshire.

Sincere thanks go to Professors Alan Dundes and Rosemary Zumwalt for their valuable advice and to Cheryl Branz, who patiently typed and retyped an earlier version of this work. An extra special thank-you goes to my sister, Heather, and her husband, Robert Fletcher, for providing the computer so necessary to the completion of this work.

I am grateful to Professor Emeritus Joel M. Halpern of the University of Massachusetts at Amherst for his contribution of remarkable photographs. For additional photographs, I am indebted to my friend, Ottilie Tosković. Finally, I wish to thank Mate Maras, Minister Counselor of the Embassy of the Republic of Croatia, who offered materials and took an active interest in the project.

Bonnie C. Marshall, 2001

Introduction

Bonnie C. Marshall

Situated between three continents—Europe, Asia, and Northern Africa—the Balkan Peninsula has experienced the migrations and invasions of many peoples from surrounding areas. Thus, the heart of the Balkan Peninsula, in southeastern Europe, is populated by a wide variety of people from different ethnic groups. These groups differ in their customs, religions, languages, and values. At times, the twenty-five nationalities living there have coexisted in peace and harmony, but disagreements have erupted periodically among them and created instability and even wars.[1] The historical amalgam of Roman, Byzantine, Slavic, Ottoman, and Austro-Hungarian cultures that creates a milieu for conflict also provides the area with cultural riches and seemingly endless fascination and color.

Both the diversity and the unity of these peoples are reflected in their folklore. Folklore, in turn, is a medium by which traditional values and information are transmitted to new generations.

BACKGROUND AND ORIGINS

Today, five independent countries are located at the heart of the Balkan Peninsula. They are Croatia and Slovenia to the west, Bosnia and Herzegovina (one country) in the center, and Yugoslavia and Macedonia to the east.

Yugoslavia can be further divided into regions with Serbia at its center, Montenegro to the southwest, Vojvodina to the north, and Kosovo and Metohija to the south. Modern Croatia is composed of Slavonia to the north, Istria to the west near Italy, and Dalmatia on the coast of the Adriatic Sea. The coastline of the Adriatic Sea is shared by Croatia, Montenegro, and Bosnia and Herzegovina.

Yugoslavia and the Balkan States

Influences

Culturally, Croatia and Slovenia have a Western, or European, orientation. People living in Croatia are called Croats, and people living in Slovenia are referred to as Slovenes. These people are of South Slavic origin. Roman Catholicism is the predominant religion, and they have adopted the Latin alphabet and Roman law. Their cultural traditions were shaped under the rule of Austria–Hungary and the Hapsburg dynasty, as well as under the brief rule of Venice and the Frankish Empire.[2]

Yugoslavia and Macedonia, on the other hand, were influenced by the Byzantine and Ottoman Turkish Empires. Their religious heritage is Eastern Orthodox Christianity and Islam. They use the Cyrillic alphabet, which was based on the Greek alphabet. Their legal and political institutions resemble those of their former Byzantine and Ottoman rulers. The majority of people living in Yugoslavia, which includes Montenegro and Macedonia, are South Slavs. A Slavic people called the Serbs form the largest segment of the population and are predominantly Orthodox Christians. Albanians, concentrated in the Kosovo region, are largely Muslim. Hungarians, Romanians, and Romanies (or Gypsies) are represented, too. Most, but not all, Montenegrins consider themselves to be Serbs and are sometimes referred to as "Mountain Serbs." In addition, Montenegro is home to a minority of Muslims and Albanians.

Old bridge across the Black River (Crna Rijeka) in Montenegro.
Photograph by Joel M. Halpern.

Bosnia and Herzegovina, situated in the middle of two very different cultures, fell under the influence of both the European west and the Byzantine and Ottoman east. In Bosnia, Serbs belong to the Orthodox religion, Muslims to the Muslim religion, and Croats to the Catholic religion. There is a tendency for Bosnian Croats and Muslims to use the Latin alphabet and for Bosnian Serbs to use the Cyrillic alphabet. Turkish, European, and Mediterranean cultures have all left their marks in Bosnia, as testified to by its architecture and cuisine. At times, this interesting religious and cultural mosaic of peoples has unraveled and erupted in violence.

Ancient Times

The story of these countries and of the diversity of peoples living there begins very long ago in 3500 B.C. when several tribes of pastoral peoples moved from the Russian steppes to the Balkan Peninsula.[3] One of the tribes, called Illyrians, settled in the western and coastal areas of the peninsula, which came to be called Illyria. Today Albanians claim the Illyrians as their ancestors.

The Illyrians were joined on the coast of the Adriatic Sea by a colorful array of traders, settlers, and pioneering people in search of land. Greek and Celtic colonists were among them. For a brief period in the fourth century, Philip II of Macedon and his son Alexander the Great appropriated territory on the Balkan Peninsula. Present-day Macedonia, whose name is derived from *Macedon*, is closely connected with Alexander's empire and with Byzantine political and cultural influences. In addition, an ancient warrior people called Thracians from Thrace, a region located on the eastern side of the Balkan Peninsula, and from Dacia, which corresponds to modern Romania, gained control, during the first millennium B.C., of sections of present-day Serbia and Macedonia.

Rome, Byzantium, and the Slavs

The Roman Empire expanded into the Balkan Peninsula at the end of the third century B.C. Although the Illyrians resisted Roman expansion, they eventually were conquered in A.D. 9. Their land, located in modern Slovenia, Croatia, Bosnia, and Montenegro, became known under Roman rule as Illyricum. Serbia fell to the Romans in 29 B.C., and Roman territories in Serbia and Macedonia became known as Moesia. The name of Skopje, Macedonia's capital, is Roman in origin.

In the third century A.D., Rome lost control of these areas when semi-nomadic peoples challenged its authority. Germanic Goths, Asiatic Huns and Avars, Bulgars (ancestors of today's Bulgarians), and other warlike peoples weakened Rome's hold, thus allowing Byzantium with its Greek culture to expand into the Balkans.

By the sixth and seventh centuries, Slavic tribes began to settle in the Balkans on Byzantine lands. One of these tribes, the Croats, settled along the Adriatic Sea and merged with the people then living on the territory of present-day Croatia and Slovenia. The Croats eventually adopted Catholicism after 1054.

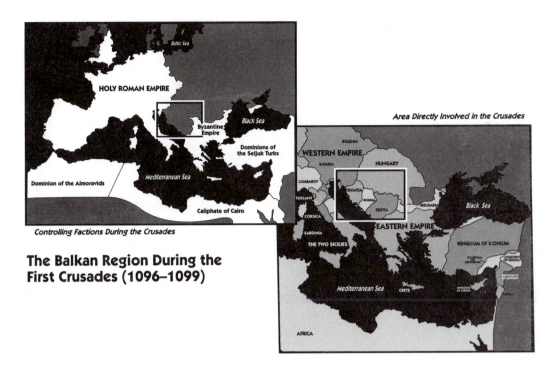

Controlling Factions During the Crusades

The Balkan Region During the First Crusades (1096–1099)

Area Directly Involved in the Crusades

Another Slavic tribe, the Serbs, allied themselves with the Byzantine emperor Heraclius and drove the Avars and Bulgars away. Thereafter, they settled in the areas of present-day Montenegro, Serbia, and Macedonia.

Bosnia was split between Croats in the central, northern, and western areas, and Serbs in the east and to the south in Herzegovina. This division placed Bosnia at a cultural crossroads.

The Medieval Period

For Serbs and Montenegrins, the family unit defined work and relationships. People were organized in extended families, or *zadruge*, which were ruled by a chieftain, or *župan*. Members of a *zadruga* owned and farmed the land. The first Serbian state, which was known as Raška, can be traced to the ninth century and was located in today's eastern Montenegro and southern Serbia.

The family of Stefan Nemanja, who was crowned "King of Serbia, Dalmatia, and Bosnia" in 1168, ruled Serbian lands for two centuries. Under Nemanjić rule, Serbia entered a golden age. Stefan Dušan (1331–1355) expanded the Nemanjić territory to include lands in modern Albania, Montenegro, Macedonia, and parts of Greece, Bosnia, and Serbia. In the thirteenth century an independent Orthodox church, separate from the church of Constantinople, was established. Churches and monasteries were built and were especially numerous in Kosovo and Metohija, an area in southern Yugoslavia.

In the ninth century, Bulgaria controlled lands from the Black Sea to the Adriatic Sea. The Bulgarian capital was in Ohrid, which is now located in western Macedonia. The Byzantine Empire wrested power briefly, but Bulgaria regained control of Macedonia from 1185 to the fourteenth century when Serbia's Stefan Dušan was crowned emperor in the city of Skopje, the capital of modern Macedonia.

In medieval times, rule in Bosnia changed hands many times. Bosnia was ruled by the Byzantine Empire, then annexed by Hungary into a Serbian kingdom. However, from 1180 to 1463 a Bosnian state existed and even managed to incorporate Herzegovina to its south, as well as a small piece of land in Dalmatia on the Adriatic Sea. An independent Bosnian church was founded. It was a branch of the Catholic church, which had fallen under the influence of Orthodoxy.

Mosque and market view in Banja Luka, Bosnia. The mosque was destroyed during the recent civil war.

Photograph by Joel M. Halpern.

When the Frankish empire disintegrated in the tenth century, Germans gained control of the Slovenian state, and the Slovenes became serfs, or slaves, who were called Wends by the Germans. In the thirteenth and fourteenth centuries, Slovenia was seized by the Austrian Hapsburgs and a feudal system of estates run by local noblemen was established. The Slovenes were forced to accept Austrian and German customs and traditions, and they became members of the Roman Catholic Church. The Ottoman Turkish Empire never penetrated Slovenia. As a result, Slovenes lived thereafter in relative peace under the influence of western Europe.

Slovenia's neighbor to the east, medieval Croatia, maintained its independence until 1102 when it came under Hungarian rule. However, the Croatian nobility was allowed to keep its lands and privileges. Over the years Croatia's borders shifted. Its territory in Dalmatia on the Adriatic Sea was lost first to Venice in the fifteenth century and later to the Ottoman Empire. In the sixteenth century, power passed from the Hungarians to the Austrian Hapsburgs, who attempted to defend what remained of Croatia from attack by the Ottoman Turks by creating a zone called the Military Frontier. The Military Frontier (*Vojna Krajina*) was populated by Serbian refugees who had been driven to the north by the Ottomans, thereby creating a large Serbian minority in Croatia.

The Ottoman Turkish Empire

After the twilight of the Nemanjić dynasty in Serbia, weak clan leaders fought for control. The Ottoman Empire saw an opportunity to push into the heart of the Balkans. The decisive battle occurred in 1389 on Kosovo Field, where the Ottomans defeated the Serbs and their allies. Kosovo Field (widely sung about in epic folk songs) and the area surrounding it have become a holy land in the hearts of the Serbs and have deep meaning in their national consciousness.

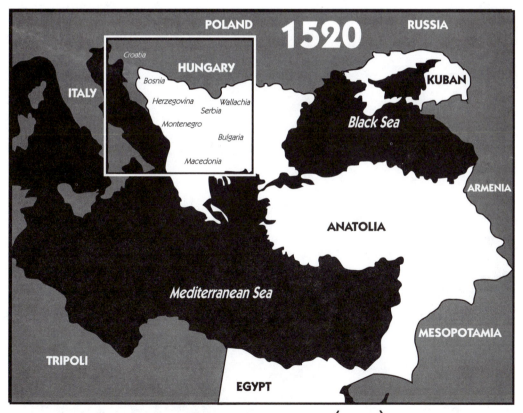

Balkan Region of the Ottoman Empire (1520)

Thereafter, Serbia became a vassal of the Ottomans, paying taxes and submitting to Turkish governance for 500 years. The Turkish sultans ruled with an iron hand, and all rebellions were met with instant retaliation. Many Serbs moved out of the Kosovo region, retreating from the Turks, and the void was filled by Albanians who came into the area and displaced the Serbs. The Ottomans retained their control until the nineteenth century.

In 1804 Karadjordje ("Black George") led a rebellion against the Turks, whose elite corps, called Janissaries, were plundering the people. Karadjordje was defeated, and a punitive reign of terror ensued. Not far from the town of Niš, Skull Tower (*Cele Kula*), constructed by Turks to commemorate a nineteenth-century victory and composed of the heads of slain Serbs, stands as a memorial to Serb suffering under the Ottoman rule.[4]

Finally, in 1815 Prince (*knez*) Miloš Obrenović led another rebellion, which eventually drove the Turks out of Serbia, and in 1830, Serbia was granted independence. The Ottoman stranglehold on the Balkans was weakening.

Macedonia, too, came under Ottoman control by the end of the fourteenth century, although it was the fifteenth century before Byzantium and its capital, Constantinople, fell to the Ottomans.[5] Ultimately, the Balkan Peninsula was freed from the Turks as a result of the Balkan War of 1912. The war was conducted by an alliance of Serbia, Bulgaria, Montenegro, and Greece. At its end, the territories of Macedonia were divided between Greece, Serbia, and Bulgaria. Thereafter, these

Balkan States Following the Second Baltic War (1913)

three countries vied for control and attempted to assimilate the Macedonians. Turkish rulers and landowners were either expelled or displaced by war.

To this very day, Turkish influence can be observed in the areas that were conquered by them. Young boys between the ages of ten and twenty were converted to Islam, for example, and were trained to work in the government or in the corps of Janissaries. This practice was referred to as the "blood tax." Many Slavs converted to Islam for economic reasons, to get ahead in a Turkish-controlled economy. The Turkish system required that local agents raise money or troops for the sultan. These agents were often Islamized Slavs. Because of these policies, Macedonians, along with Bosnian Muslims, are closely connected to the Ottoman heritage.

Bosnia was divided by the Turks into districts and, together with sections of Croatia and Serbia, became a province of the Ottoman Empire, governed by a vizier, whose orders were implemented by local pashas. The weakness of the Bosnian Christian church, isolated from Rome and beset by charges of heresy, ensured the spread of Islam there. However, the Ottoman reign was far from peaceful. It was marked by periodic wars. Invasions by Austria weakened Bosnia and led to tax revolts and a decrease in the Muslim population. Nevertheless, the towns of Sarajevo (Bosnia's capital), Mostar, and Banja Luka flourished as cultural and religious centers.

The Austro-Hungarian Empire

The Ottoman Empire had invaded the Balkans from the south, whereas Austria and Hungary made incursions from the north. In 1878 at the Congress of Berlin, it was decided that Bosnia and Herzegovina would be governed as a protectorate by Austria–Hungary. Croatia, too, came under the control of the Austro–Hungarian Empire. The Hungarians attempted to assimilate both the Croats and Serbs living within Croatia's Military Frontier by encouraging hostility between the two ethnic groups. Croats responded by forming the Illyrian movement, which advocated the unification of all the South Slavs. A first step in unification was the creation of a common literary language. The Illyrian movement eventually came to be called Yugoslavism.

Part of Slovenia's territory came under the control of Napoleon I and France at the beginning of the nineteenth century. At that time, Slovenes, like Croats, espoused the ideas of the Illyrian movement. European ideas of revolution and independence began taking hold on both Slovene and Croat soil.

Serbia was granted Vojvodina, a piece of land to the north, as a reward for supporting the Austrian Hapsburg emperor in 1848–1849. Vojvodina remained under Austrian rule until 1867 when control reverted to Hungary. Hungary soon began a campaign to assimilate the Serbs, too.

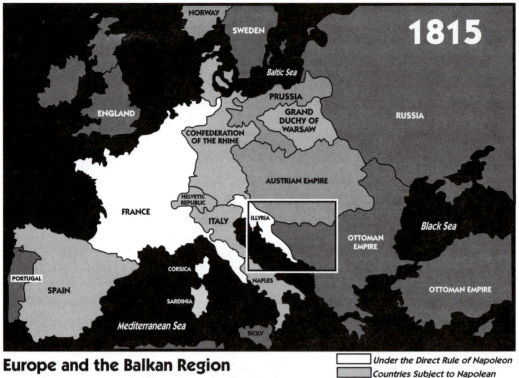

Europe and the Balkan Region Under Napoleonic Conquests (1815)

Under the Direct Rule of Napoleon
Countries Subject to Napolean
Countries Allied with Napoloen

The Two World Wars and the Emergence of Yugoslavia

World War I was precipitated by the assassination of the Austrian Archduke Francis Ferdinand in 1914 in Sarajevo, the capital of Bosnia. This marked the demise of the Austro–Hungarian Empire. In 1918, the Kingdom of Serbs, Croats, and Slovenes was formed out of the ashes of war. The Kingdom included the South Slavic territories of Serbia, Montenegro, Croatia, Slovenia, Bosnia and Herzegovina, and a partitioned Macedonia. In 1929, the name of this country was changed to Yugoslavia.

World War II introduced a period of violence and instability. In 1941, Yugoslavia was invaded by the Axis powers and was quickly defeated by German troops. Germany and Italy promptly set up puppet governments there. Sections of Yugoslavia were carved up and divided between Germany, Italy, Bulgaria, and Hungary. Montenegro and Serbia resisted the Axis powers spiritedly. Their losses were great. Montenegro alone lost a quarter of its population.

A resistance movement under the leadership of Colonel Draža Mihailović was formed. The members of this movement were called Chetniks. After Hitler attacked the Soviet Union, Josip Broz, a Croat–Slovene Communist who became known as Tito, led another resistance group called the Partisans. These two groups fought one another. Tito, supported by the Soviet Union's Red Army, ultimately gained the upper hand and the rule of Yugoslavia. He ordered the execution of Mihailović and his supporters and exterminated all opponents.

Yugoslavia emerged from World War II as a communist federation of six republics headed by Tito. The six republics were Slovenia, Croatia, Bosnia and Herzegovina, Serbia, Montenegro, and Macedonia. In adopting Communism, a socialist system of governance where property is owned in common, Yugoslavia became a member of the Soviet bloc, which included the Soviet Union and its satellite nations. However, Tito valued his independence, and the Yugoslav form of Communism was moderate in comparison to that prevalent in other Soviet bloc nations. For this reason, Yugoslavia was expelled from the Soviet bloc in 1948.

Tito created two autonomous areas within Serbia—Vojvodina and Kosovo–Metohija. Even before the end of World War II, Albanians living in Kosovo revolted in support of the unification of Kosovo with Albania. This desire of the Albanians for independence persisted and eventually erupted in civil war in 1998.

The Fall of Communism

In the early 1990s, as Communism collapsed in the Soviet Union and the Soviet bloc nations, the concept of a united nation of South Slavs also disintegrated. Five of the six republics demanded independence and became separate countries, leaving only Serbia and Montenegro united in the Federal Republic of Yugoslavia.

Without Communism and the iron hand of Tito, who died in 1980, instability and ethnic hostilities escalated.[6] A territorial struggle arose between the Yugoslav government, headed by President Slobodan Milošević, and ethnic Albanians, who wanted to establish their own rule in Yugoslav Kosovo. In 1990, the Albanians proclaimed a Republic of Kosovo. Religious differences (most Albanians are Muslim and most Serbs are Orthodox Christian) fueled the battle.[7]

Albanians cited demographic predominance and longevity of habitation as descendents of ancient Illyrians as reasons they should be given autonomy.[8] Serbs, on the other hand, claimed that the area was of historical importance to them and represented a national treasure of deep emotional, cultural, and architectural significance, containing, as it does, Kosovo Field, the national shrine where Serbia fell to the Turks in 1389.

In 1999, NATO authorized air strikes against the Milošević regime in an attempt to end the violence and return Kosovar Albanian refugees to their homes. Air operations were suspended later that year and a security force was sent to Kosovo under the auspices of the United Nations to keep order and rebuild the once beautiful area. The task has been difficult because hostilities have not abated.[9] Montenegro, as part of the Yugoslav federation, has supported the Yugoslav government and Milošević regarding his Kosovo policy, but it has kept a low profile. Currently, there are rumblings concerning its succession from the federation.

THE FEDERAL REPUBLIC OF YUGOSLAVIA

CROATIA

Meanwhile, Croatia had declared its independence in 1991. In 1992, after a civil war had been waged between Croats and ethnic Serbs living in Croatia, the Republic of Croatia became a member of the United Nations.[10] The Republic of Slovenia, too, declared its independence in 1991.[11]

SLOVENIA

The Republic of Bosnia and Herzegovina passed a referendum for independence in 1992 that resulted in the outbreak of fighting among Bosnian Orthodox Serbs, Catholic Croats, and Muslims. Hostilities were exacerbated by cultural and religious differences. The world watched in dismay as the once beautiful city of Sarajevo, the country's capital and home of the 1984 Winter Olympics, was almost completely destroyed during the conflict between Bosnian Serbs and Muslims. Meanwhile, Bosnian Croats destroyed the city of Mostar's famed ancient fairy-tale bridge named *Stari Most*.

Fighting abated only after the 1995 Dayton Peace Accord divided Bosnia into sections policed by the United States, the United Kingdom, and France. Bosnian Serbs have their own Serbian Republic, while Croats and Muslims are in the Federation of Bosnia and Herzegovina. There is also a central government, the Republic of Bosnia and Herzegovina, to manage matters of mutual concern.[12] Meanwhile, people of all ethnic groups have suffered, and the destruction has saddened the world.

BOSNIA and HERZEGOVINA

Macedonia, the last country to free itself from the Ottoman Turks, developed a national consciousness rather late. Only after World War II ended were an alphabet and a standardized grammar written, and a university established. This factor ensured the lively and lengthy existence of an oral tradition. Macedonia, too, declared its independence from Yugoslavia in 1991 and has since had to play a delicate diplomatic role in the Balkans.[13] The country has been faced by internal ethnic tensions between Macedonians and Albanians, the influx of refugees from war-torn Kosovo and Bosnia, and the emergence of ancient hostilities in Greece's objection to the use of the ancient Hellenic name *Macedonia* to designate a non-Greek territory.

Recent developments have included the fall of Slobodan Milošević of Yugoslavia, who lost the September 2000 presidential election to Vojislav Koštunica. In March of 2001, Milošević was arrested for war crimes. Although President Koštunica's victory was celebrated in Yugoslavia and the West, trouble erupted in Macedonia. On March 14, 2001, Kosovar Albanian rebels invaded Macedonia with the intention of expanding their territory.

Balkan history is complex and constantly evolving. Sadly, there seems to be no end to ethnic hostilities and no hope of the Balkans achieving stability in the near future.

MACEDONIA

ORAL LITERATURE

The stormy history of the former Yugoslavia has guaranteed the existence of its folklore through modern times. Buffeted over the years by political upheavals, religious differences, and attacks by Romans, Byzantines, Bulgars, Franks, and Turks; occupied for centuries by the Ottoman Turkish Empire and Austria–Hungary; and fragmented today by internal strife, the land known until recently as Yugoslavia has had little opportunity for the normal development of a written literature. Under these circumstances literature was preserved for a long time in oral form, with belles lettres evolving quite late (as late as post World War II in the case of Macedonia), not only because of the constant turmoil but because the conquerors, for the most part, did not foster indigenous cultures. Rather, the conquering empires attempted to assimilate the South Slavs into their respective cultures.

Folk Poetry

Epic poems are common throughout the Balkans. They serve as a means of preserving history orally and passing it on to future generations. Sung by bards called *guslari* to the accompaniment of a primitive, one-stringed instrument called a *gusle*, they portray a glorious history and reveal the indomitable will of a people who refused to let their oppressors break their spirit.[14] Epic poetry celebrates the daring heroes of the past, both Christian and Muslim.

The singer of epic poetry improvises and adjusts the length of his song to the audience's interest. Usually, the songs are sung during breaks at work or during leisure time at a local inn or café.

Folk Prose

Historically, scholars have given a great deal of attention to the oral tradition of folk songs (*narodne pjesme*), particularly epic songs. Folk prose (*narodna proza*), which is the focus of this collection, has been neglected by comparison. This is interesting because whereas folk songs are connected to a sense of national pride and have a concrete historical character, folktales display universal motifs and have a more general appeal. The hero or heroine is frequently nameless, and the action takes place in an unknown magical land inhabited by supernatural beings and objects. The hero is everyman, and the heroine is everywoman.

In these stories, a delicate lyricism is sometimes combined with shocking events. The juxtaposition of the poetic with cruel reality makes a lasting impression on readers. Of course, good always triumphs in the end.

The Contribution of
Vuk Stefanović Karadžić

No account of the folktale, regardless of how brief, can fail to mention the name of Vuk Stefanović Karadžić (1787–1864).[15] Germany has its Brothers Grimm, Russia its Aleksandr Afanasyev, and Yugoslavia its Vuk Karadžić. Born a Serbian peasant, he is considered the most influential Serbian writer of the nineteenth century. He adapted the Cyrillic alphabet to the form still used today. Not only did he contribute to the development of Serbia's literary language, but he played an instrumental role in the collection and preservation of the area's rich oral heritage. Although he lost one of his legs and was later exiled by his government, for many years he traveled throughout the countryside assiduously recording folk songs, folktales, riddles, and proverbs.

ABOUT THE TALES

Russian scholars divide folktales into three main categories: animal tales, fairy (or magical) tales, and tales of everyday life. For the purposes of this collection, the Russian paradigm works well, but I have added "Myths and Legends" as an additional category because these genres reflect the essence of the Balkan cultures that created them and present an opportunity for a better understanding of those cultures. Russian scholars do not include myths and legends in their definition of the folktale because myths and legends do not represent pure fantasy, a criterion for the Russian folktale. Rather, legends and myths contain elements of reality and are frequently based on an actual event or fact and/or are reflective of ritual.

Myths and Legends

The category titled "Myths and Legends" contains explanatory stories that are distinguished by the presence of mythological characters. "Why Man Lives Eighty Years" and "Nasta and the Sun" are pourquoi tales explaining the evolution of man's life span and the naming of the swallow respectively. Also included are legends containing local lore about hidden treasure ("The Miser and the Generous Man"), the prosperity of a village ("The Little Shepherd"), and the story of a mythical family ("Tsar Dukljan").

"Beautiful Mara," a Macedonian tale, exhibits borrowings from the Greek Psyche myth. Mara, like Psyche, is warned not to attempt to find out who her lover is. Mara, too, lights a candle in order to see her beloved's face, spilling drops of wax onto his face and awakening him. Like Psyche, Mara has to go in search of her mate. Both heroines are given tasks to fulfill that require a display of patience before they can be reunited with their true loves. However, Mara's tasks differ from Psyche's and are in accordance with a Slavic motif; she must wear out a pair of iron shoes and carry an iron staff during her search for her husband.

All but two of these tales display pagan elements, as indicated by the presence of deities. The devils in "The Miser and the Generous Man" belong to the category of evil spirits (*nečiste sile*). The Sun is personified and regarded as a god in "Nasta and the Sun." Gods frequently adopt human traits, much as they do in Greek mythology, so the Sun falls in love with Nasta, a mortal.

Perhaps the most intriguing lesser deity is the *vila*, who inhabits forests, wells, lakes, glens, and mountains. She has a dual nature and usually acts according to what the victim or beneficiary, as the case may be, deserves. Young and lovely, robed in white, she sings like the Siren with a bewitchingly sweet voice and whiles away her time dancing a round dance, called the *kolo*. The *vila* is particularly dangerous when dancing or when crossed. If angered, she is capable of tearing out her victim's eyes (see "The Twelve Crumbs"). Present in fairy tales, as well as in mythological stories, the *vila* also helps the young and unfortunate, and like the mermaid or selkie of Irish folklore, she can marry a human. Like the Amazon of Greek lore, she carries a bow and arrow. She knows how to heal with herbs and, like the Fates, can foretell the future.

Animal Tales

Fables and tales that have animals as main characters are in the section titled "Animal Tales." In these stories, often humorous, animals display wit and teach a lesson about human behavior. The lesson is almost always implicit. When the message is explicit—as it is in "The Mouse and the Ant," which ends with the adage "greed always leads to grief"—the story takes on a didactic flavor and can more properly be called a fable.

"The Little Hedgehog," "Bey Zlatum," and "The Snake Bridegroom" contain elements of the fairy tale and display remnants of totemic belief. The transformation of animals into people and people into animals rises from an ancient worldview. Janček the hedgehog, like the Frog Prince, turns out to be a handsome young man in disguise.

Auntie Fox in "Bey Zlatum" is a Balkan "Puss in Boots." Byelorussians, too, tell a variant of this tale. As in the English version, the Byelorussian hero is a cat, not a fox. In the South Slavic version, Auntie adopts the role of helper when she rewards the poor man who spares her life after he catches her stealing his meager supply of grain.

An important aspect of this story is the information it gives about wedding customs. Auntie Fox plays the role of matchmaker, and indeed matchmakers were common in southeastern Europe. They negotiated on behalf of the groom, usually for a fee. If the father of the prospective bride agreed, a meeting was arranged during which the young people were asked if they were agreeable to the marriage. If the bride lived in a distant village, the wedding procession had to travel to fetch her. Such is the situation when Auntie Fox instructs Bey Zlatum to roll in a puddle before their arrival at the bride's home so that the bride's family will be tricked into believing that many members of the wedding procession have drowned. The firing of pistols, a foreign custom to Westerners who connect shooting with war and violence, indicates festive rejoicing in the story. It was common practice for guests to set out for church firing pistols, so guests leave Bey Zlatum's home firing shots into the air to express their joy.

The wedding customs depicted in "Bey Zlatum" lasted well into the twentieth century, and some variation of them is still practiced today. Industrialization and the exodus of young people to urban areas in search of work has led to modernization and to the subsequent loss of many village traditions, except in remote rural areas.

Fairy Tales

Hypnotic daggers, evil stepmothers, devils that can change form, beautiful tsarevnas, prophetic birds—these are the romantic fare of the fairy, or magical, tale.

The fairy tale (*bajka*) narrates the adventures of a hero or heroine. Typically the hero ignores a prohibition and is punished by falling into evil hands. He undergoes certain tests or fights a battle with the aid of magic helpers in the fairy-tale realm, then returns to the reality of his world with a reward, frequently a bride, that he acquired for the successful completion of the tests set before him.[16]

With regard to the heroine, the tale conveys social expectations concerning women's behavior and roles. The passive beauty lacks autonomy, must be rescued by the hero, and serves as the hero's prize. The pasha's daughter in "The Young Man and His Vampire Brother" is an example. She is a mere fixture, lying in her coffin for most of the narrative, and is given to the hero as a reward for his breaking a magic spell.

Other models reflect a pre-Christian culture, in which women were strong, independent, and in command of their fate. In the tale "The Shepherd and the Three Vilas," the golden-haired *vila*, a pagan lesser deity with magical powers, is an example of a heroine who flees marriage, preferring the freedom of her matriarchy to marriage within the patriarchy.

The dragon is a symbol of paganism, a representative of ancient beliefs that predated Christianity and were difficult for the clergy to eradicate. The dragon is usually evil and ravages the countryside, but sometimes is depicted as kind and helpful. The dragoness in "You Reap What You Sow" is an example of the latter. Reflecting paganism in a positive guise as Mistress of the Forest, she rewards the heroine, who proves to be a willing pupil of the ancient arts and who will transmit the dragoness's secret knowledge to a new generation.

Tales of Everyday Life

The last category of stories contains tales of everyday life. These merry tales reveal the wisdom and humor of the folk. In a scathing exposure of human foibles, the little man triumphs over the powerful. In "Ero and the Turk," for instance, the Serb dares to mock his Turkish oppressor. "It's Not Easy to Steal from a Gypsy" is a clever inversion of the destructive stereotype that depicts Gypsies as thieving cutthroats. Nasradin Hodja is a character popular among people of the East. Nasreddin Afandi, or Efendi, the counterpart of Nasradin Hodja, is to be found in the folklore of Tadzhikistan.

A list of sources from which these stories were taken is available at the end of the book. For those interested in reading more about South Slavic and Balkan folklore, an excellent bibliography can be found in *Yugoslav Literature in English*.[17] In addition, a list is provided on pages xl–xli.

Watching the sheep in the glen.
Photograph by Joel M. Halpern.

Peasant houses in Vojvodina.
Photography by Joel M. Halpern.

A Turkish-style home and traditional Albanian tower house (on the right) in Kosovo.

Photograph by Joel M. Halpern.

Trogir, a town in Croatia on the Adriatic Sea.
Photograph by Joel M. Halpern.

LANGUAGES AND TRANSLATIONS

The former Yugoslavia had three official languages: Serbo–Croatian, Slovenian, and Macedonian. Now that most of the former republics have ceded and formed independent countries, there is an objection to the use of the name *Serbo–Croatian* to indicate the languages of Serbia and Croatia. It is preferred that they be called Serbian and Croatian respectively, although the languages have a great deal in common. There are three variants of Serbo–Croatian—Shtokavian, Chakavian, and Kajkavian—named after the word for "what" in each of the dialects. Primarily, the Croatian and Serbian literary languages are based on the Shtokavian dialect. The Chakavian dialect is spoken in northern Dalmatia and the islands of the Adriatic Sea. The Kajkavian dialect has a resemblance to Slovenian and is spoken west of Zagreb, the capital of Croatia.

In addition, two alphabets are in use, the Latin alphabet and the Cyrillic alphabet. Ninth-century Greek missionaries, Cyril and Methodius, are credited with the creation of the ancestor of today's Cyrillic alphabet, which was named in honor of Cyril. It is modeled on the Greek alphabet and bears a resemblance to it.

Generally speaking, the Latin alphabet is used in the west (Slovenia and Croatia), while the Cyrillic alphabet is used in the east (Serbia and Montenegro). Macedonia, too, uses a Cyrillic-based alphabet. In Bosnia and Herzegovina, located in the center of the former Yugoslavia, both alphabets are used.

In translating, the differences in the alphabets presented no particular problem. The dialects, however, did. Folklore, in particular, retains colloquialisms and regional turns of phrases. Unless the translator is working with a literary version of a tale, the language is not standard and can pose problems.

In addition, context is extremely important in these languages, and a word can have various meanings and connotations depending upon its use and position in a sentence. Suffice it to say that I have done the best that I can to render a comprehensible, accurate translation and retelling. The small number of tales included here that were taken from a Russian collection of South Slavic folklore have already undergone a degree of reinterpretation in their initial translation from Serbian into Russian.

When transliterating, or rendering words in English, I used the Library of Congress specifications. In addition, a glossary of names and words with English meanings and pronunciations is included.

Because folktale heroes have universal characteristics and therefore could be anyone, even you or I, tellers give them common names or fail to name them at all. When appropriate, I have honored their anonymity. If I considered it an irritating detraction, I gave the character a name. The choice was subjective and my own.

In the telling, folktales frequently lack detail and elaboration because knowledge of the cultural context of the tales is assumed by the teller. When tales are told in a culture different than that for which the tale was intended, cultural knowledge cannot be taken for granted. Therefore, I have retold or adapted many of my translations, filling in the gaps with explanations and elaborations. I must take full responsibility for the retellings and adaptations. No drastic changes have been made. The basic structure and sequence of events remains intact. My contribution has consisted mainly of providing motivation, description, and characterization where the bareness of the original narrative required further embellishment to be comprehensible and aesthetically enjoyable to the reader.

Below its title, each tale bears a designation of the country it is from and the region of the country, if known. Exceptions are the Albanian and Romany (or Gypsy) stories, which are told by these peoples living in the former Yugoslavia.

The photographs, which were selected to depict children and adults at work and at play in the Balkans, reflect the traditions and cultures of five countries (Yugoslavia, Croatia, Bosnia and Herzegovina, Slovenia, and Macedonia). The oldest photographs date back to the 1950s.

NOTES

1.   For a good summary of the history, geography, people, government, economics, religion, and culture of the former Yugoslavia, consult Glen E. Curtis, ed., *Yugoslavia, A Country Study* (Federal Research Division of the Library of Congress, preliminary drafts). Available: http://lcweb2.loc.gov/frd/cs/yutoc.html. (Accessed April 23, 2001).

2.   The Frankish Empire extended over modern-day France, Germany, and Italy.

3.   For a concise history of the Balkans, see *The New Encyclopaedia Britannica*, 15th ed., s.v. "Balkan States," from which the history here was reconstructed.

4.   Niš is a Serbian town located northeast of Priština and southeast of Belgrade.

5.   A timeline of important events from 653 B.C. through 1995 can be found on the Internet. See "Chronology of Macedonian History" in *Makedonski Icelenuchki Almanac '97*. (Matitsa na Icelenitsite od Makedonija, Skopje, 1997). Available: http://www .geocities.com/~makedonija/chrono.html. (Accessed June 21, 2001).

6.   A good analysis of ethnic tensions and conflicts in the Balkans can be found in *Neighbors at War, Anthropological Perspectives on Yugoslav Ethnicity, Culture, and History*, edited by Joel M. Halpern and David A. Kideckel (University Park, Pennsylvania State University Press, 2000).

7. Long ago most Albanians were Catholic, but they converted to Islam under Turkish rule.

8. For an understanding of the economic poverty that drove Albanians from their country into neighboring areas in Yugoslavia and Macedonia, see Dusko Doder, "Albania Opens the Door," *National Geographic* 182, no. 1 (July 1992): 66–93. It is an account of a man returning to his homeland, Albania, the poorest country in Europe.

9. For a brief account chronicling NATO's involvement in Kosovo, see s.v. "Yugoslavia" in *The World Almanac and Book of Facts,* 2001 ed.

10. For a brief, well-written history of Croatia, see "A Short History of Croatia" in *Croatia Tourist Guide* (Lexicographic Institute Miroslav Krleža, Zagreb, 1998). Available: http://www.htz.hr/history.htm. (Accessed Jan. 26, 2000).

11. Students will enjoy a visit to *Slovenia: A Guide to Virtual Slovenia* at http://www.matkurja.com/. This is a creative, informative Internet site. Mother Hen (*mat' kurja*) is the central graphic. The visitor clicks on her eggs to access information. Clicking on the egg titled "Country Info" leads to the option of "Slovenian History in Brief," a historical timeline extending from the end of the sixth century to the present.

12. For a thorough account of the war in Bosnia, see Priit J. Vesilind, "In Focus: Bosnia," *National Geographic* 189, no. 6 (June 1996): 48–61.

13. For an article chronicling recent events in historical context, see Priit J. Vesilind, "Macedonia: Caught in the Middle," *National Geographic* 189, no. 3 (March 1996): 118–39.

14. To learn more about the *guslari* and epic songs, see Albert Bates Lord, *The Singer of Tales* (Cambridge, Harvard University Press, 1960) and *Epic Singers and Oral Tradition: Myth and Poetics* (Ithaca, Cornell University Press, 1991). See also, Mary L. Lord, ed., *The Singer Resumes the Tale: Myth and Poetics* (Ithaca, Cornell University Press, 1995).

15. For an account of Karadžić's life and influence on the shaping of language and literature, see Duncan Wilson, *The Life and Times of Vuk Stefanović Karadžić (1787–1864): Literacy, Literature and National Independence* (Ann Arbor, Michigan, Slavic Publications, 1986).

16. Vladimir Propp made the claim that all fairy tales can be morphologically deduced from the basic one involving the heroine being abducted by a villain. He created a single formula, composed of functional units, for all fairy tales. See V. Propp, *Morphology of the Folktale,* trans. Laurence Scott, 2d ed. (Austin, University of Texas Press, 1977).

17.   Mihailovich, Vasa D., and Mateja Matejić, eds. *Yugoslav Literature in English: A Bibliography of Translations and Criticism, 1921–1975.* (Cambridge, MA, Slavica, 1976).

ADDITIONAL SOURCES

History and People

Allcock, John B. *Explaining Yugoslavia.* New York: Columbia University Press, 2000.

Andrić, Ivo. *The Development of Spiritual Life in Bosnia Under the Influence of Turkish Rule.* Ed. Želimir B. Jurčić and John F. Loud. Durham: Duke University Press, 1990.

Carmichael, Cathie, and James Gow. *Slovenia and the Slovenes: A Small State and the New Europe.* London: Hurst and Company, 2000.

Ceh, Nick, and Jeff Harder. *The Golden Apple: War and Democracy in Croatia and Bosnia.* East European Monographs 450. New York: Columbia University Press, 1996.

Costa, Nicholas J. *Shattered Illusions: Albania, Greece and Yugoslavia.* East European Monographs 520. New York: Columbia University Press, 1998.

Dragnich, Alex N., ed. *Serbia's Historical Heritage.* East European Monographs 347. New York: Columbia University Press, 1994.

Duijzings, Gerlachus. *Religion and the Politics of Identity in Kosovo.* New York: Columbia University Press, 2000.

Elsie, Robert. *Kosovo: In the Heart of the Powder Keg.* East European Monographs 478. New York: Columbia University Press, 1997.

Harris, Nathaniel. *The War in Former Yugoslavia.* New Perspectives Series. Chatham, NJ: Raintree Steck-Vaughn, 1998.

Hupchick, Dennis P. *The Balkans from Constantinople to Communism.* New York: Palgrave, 2001.

Lampe, John R. *Yugoslavia As History: Twice There Was a Country.* 2d ed. New York: Cambridge University Press, 2000.

Poulton, Hugh. *Who Are the Macedonians?* 2d ed. Bloomington: Indiana University Press, 2000.

———. *Muslim Identity and the Balkan States*. Washington Square, NY: New York University Press in Association with the Islamic Council, 1997.

Ristelhueber, René. *History of the Balkan Peoples*. Ed. and trans. Sherman D. Spector. New York: Twayne Publishers, 1971.

Rody, Maryn. *The Breakup of Yugoslavia*. Conflicts Series. New York: Silver Burdett Press, 1994.

Singleton, Frederick Bernard. *A Short History of the Yugoslav Peoples*. New York: Cambridge University Press, 1985.

Folklore

Barac, Antun. *A History of Yugoslav Literature*. Trans. Petar Mijušković. The Joint Committee on Eastern Europe Publications Series. Ann Arbor: Michigan Slavic Publications, 1973.

Durham, Mary Edith. "Albanian and Montenegrin Folklore." *Folk-Lore* 23 (1912): 224–29.

Sazdov, Tomé. "Origins and Classifications of Macedonian Folk Prose." *Macedonian Review* 43.2 (1988): 141–56.

Zoltowski, Adam. "Folklore: Yugoslavia." *Slavonic Encyclopaedia*. Ed. Joseph S. Roucek. New York: Philosophical Library, 1949.

Žunić-Baš, Leposava. *Folk Tradition in Yugoslavia: Ten Tours*. Belgrade, n.d. (1966).

Folk Poetry

Asboth, K. Janos De, ed. *An Official Tour Through Bosnia and Herzegovina*. London: Swan Sonnenschein, 1980. (Contains twenty traditional songs of Bosnian Muslims.)

Low, David Halyburton, trans. *The Ballads of Marko Kraljević*. New York: Greenwood Press, 1968.

Mügge, Maximilian A. *Serbian Folk Songs, Fairy Tales and Proverbs*. London: Drane, 1916.

Noyes, George Rapall, and Leonard Bacon, trans. *Heroic Ballads of Servia*. Boston: Sherman, French, 1913.

Rootham, Helen. *Kossovo: Heroic Songs of the Serbs*. Oxford: Blackwell, 1920.

Subotić, Dragutin P. *Yugoslav Popular Ballads: Their Origin and Development*. Cambridge: The University Press, 1932.

Folk Prose

Ackerly, Frederick George, ed. "Five Tales from Bosnia." *Journal of the Gypsy Lore Society* 23.3–4 (1944): 97–106.

Berlić-Mažuranić, Ivana. *Croatian Tales of Long Ago*. London: Ruskin House, 1924.

Cvetanovska, Danica, Irma Rosenfeld, and William Rosenfeld, trans. *The Moon in the Well and Other Macedonian Folk Tales*. New York: Greenfield Review Press, 1988.

Ćurčija-Prodanović, Nada. *Yugoslav Folk-Tales*. New York: Oxford University Press, 1957.

Davis, Chivers E. *Tales of Serbian Life*. New York: Dodd, Mead, n.d.

Djordjević, Tihomir. "Jugoslav Gypsy Folk Tales." *Slavonic Review*. Trans. Fanny Foster. 14.41 (1936): 288–93.

Kavčič, Vladmir. *The Golden Bird: Folk Tales from Slovenia*. Trans. Jan Dekker and Helen Lenček. Cleveland: The World Publishing Company, 1969.

Mijatovich, Madam Elodie L. *Serbian Fairy Tales*. London: William Heinemann, 1917.

Mijatovies, Madam Csedomille, trans. and comp. *Serbian Folk-Lore*. New York: Benjamin Blom, 1968.

Naake, John T. *Slavonic Fairy Tales: Collected and Translated from the Russian, Polish, Servian, and Bohemian*. London: Henry S. King, 1874.

Petrovitch, Woislav M. *Hero Tales and Legends of the Serbians*. New York: Frederick A. Stokes, 1914.

Strickland, W. W. *Panslavonic Folk-Lore in Four Books*. New York: B. Westermann, 1930.

New-style coffeehouse in Sarajevo. Built after the conflict in the 1990s.
Photograph by Joel M. Halpern.

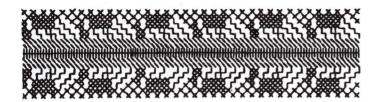

Part I

MYTHS AND LEGENDS

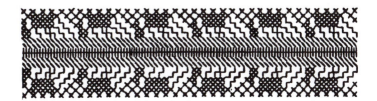

Why Man Lives Eighty Years

(Bosnia and Herzegovina)

When God created the world, He wanted to give each person only thirty years to live. "You will be tsar of all my creatures," He told Man. "You will be young, healthy, handsome, strong, and wise, and you will live for thirty years."

Ruling the earth seemed a very pleasant task to Man, but he did not like the idea of having a short life span. Still, he did not say anything to God about it.

After He created Man, God created a donkey. "You will feed on the most unappetizing food," He told the donkey, "and you will never be full. People for whom you carry heavy loads, and for whom you do services that no one else would do, will make fun of you. As a reward, they will beat you with a club without mercy. You will live thirty years."

"Lord," answered the donkey, "because I will have to suffer so many torments, thirty years seems too long for me to live. May I live only ten years?"

"You may. Let it be as you wish," God told the donkey.

When he heard this conversation, Man began squirming about. He cleared his throat and said, "Lord, please give me those twenty years that the donkey doesn't want."

"Very well, take them," God answered, "but you must take them just as they are."

Man's heart was gladdened that he had gained another twenty years of life for himself. Now he would live to be fifty years old.

Then God created a dog and said to him, "Whatever is called yours, you must defend as long as you live. You will bark at every danger you sense, and you will always sense danger while it is still far away. You will have neither sleep nor rest. You will never eat breakfast or dinner in peace, and you will always do more for others than for yourself. You, too, will live thirty years."

"Lord," said the dog, "because I must live such a troubled life, may I live only ten years?"

"Of course. Live only ten years if you wish," God replied.

Again Man cleared his throat and approached God. "Lord," he spoke out, "please give me those twenty years that the dog threw away."

"I give them to you just as they are," said God.

Again Man was glad in his heart that he had lengthened his life by another twenty years. Now he would live to be seventy years old.

Finally, God created a monkey. "You will look very much like Man," He said to him, "but you won't be Man. You will climb trees and jump from branch to branch. You will imitate what you see others do without knowing why you act that way. You, too, will live thirty years."

"Lord," said the monkey, "twenty years of such a life is enough for me. Thirty years is too much!"

"Let it be as you wish. Live twenty years," answered God.

Once again Man started scratching the back of his head. He began clearing his throat and licking his lips. Finally, he said, "Lord, please give me the ten years that the monkey doesn't want."

"You may have them. I give them to you just as they are," said God.

Man was as happy as a little child because he had gained a whole eighty years of life for himself. Everything happened according to God's word. Even today, when Man is living his own life from birth to thirty years of age, he is young, healthy, handsome, and strong. He is indeed tsar of God's creatures here on earth.

From thirty to fifty, after having married and sired children, he begins to work and worry about acquiring things, because then he is living the donkey's life.

From fifty to seventy he obtains less, but he guards what he has acquired more carefully, because then he is living the dog's life. That is why he barks like a dog at every danger that he foresees and worries constantly about being unprotected and insecure.

From seventy to eighty Man's hands shake, his legs bend, his eyes cannot see, his ears cannot hear, and his mind becomes tired and worn out. Man then enters his second childhood, and very often he truly resembles the monkey from whom he took the final ten years. ❋

Nasta and the Sun

(Slovenia)

Once upon a time there was a girl so beautiful that there was not another like her in the whole world. Her name was Nasta. One day the Sun saw her, and he fell so deeply in love with her that he stayed at the place where he had first seen her for one and a half days.

When the Sun finally came home, his mother asked him, "Where have you been for so long, dear boy?"

The Sun confessed that he had seen a beautiful girl and that he had fallen in love with her. His mother was not pleased. She scolded him for falling in love with an earthling, for it was considered a great sin for a heavenly being to want to marry a mortal.

The Sun was silent for many days, and his rays grew dim because of his misery and longing. Finally, he told his mother that he could not live without the girl.

When his mother understood how serious he was, she began feeling sorry for him. "You can get that girl easily, dear boy," she told him. "Simply lower a golden swing for her. When she is seated on it and is swinging back and forth, pull the swing up into the sky."

The Sun did as his mother advised. He made a golden swing with his bright rays and lowered it to capture the maiden.

When the people in the village where Nasta lived caught sight of it, they took turns swinging on it. Nasta and her friends came only toward evening. They began to swing back and forth. When the little maiden's turn came to sit on the golden swing, the Sun pulled it way, way up into the sky. That is how he captured Nasta and brought her to his palace.

Nasta was angry at the Sun for deceiving her. To get even with him, she pretended that she was dumb and did not know how to say anything. Finally, she began to cooperate and did whatever the Sun or his mother asked of her, but still she remained silent.

Sometimes Nasta even felt sorry for the Sun because he was sad that she did not love him. He tried to amuse her. He offered to let her ride on his golden swing, and he spent long hours begging her to utter just one word, but Nasta refused to talk to him.

Finally, the Sun lost patience with her. He got angry and told his mother to send Nasta to Auntie Death.

His mother obeyed. "Nasta, dear," she said to the little earthling, "go to Auntie Death and bring back her magic sieve. I am in great need of it."

Suspecting nothing, the little maiden set out for Auntie Death's house. When she arrived, she asked for the magic sieve.

"Please, sit down, little girl," Auntie Death chortled, pointing to a bench. "Sit down, and I'll get the sieve."

Auntie went into another room, but she was not going after the sieve. She was planning to grind her teeth to razor sharpness so that she could eat up the little girl. Nasta did not know what her intentions were, so she waited patiently for her to return.

Meanwhile, a little mouse had overheard the conversation. It approached Nasta. "Run! Quick, run!" the mouse warned her. "There's not a second to waste. Auntie Death has gone to sharpen her teeth so that she can grind you to bits and eat you up."

The mouse gave Nasta a comb and a scarf. "When Auntie Death runs after you, first throw the comb behind you, and it will grow into a thick forest.

"If Auntie Death manages to hack her way through the forest, then throw the scarf behind you, and it will become a river."

Nasta thanked the kind little mouse, gave the small creature a kiss, and ran away.

When she looked back, she saw that Auntie Death was running after her, her sharp teeth flashing.

First she threw the comb at her, and it grew into an impenetrable forest. Auntie Death hacked through the forest with her sharp teeth as if she were mowing grass.

Soon Auntie Death was about to catch up with the little girl again. Nasta threw the scarf behind her, and the scarf became a wide river.

Auntie Death picked up her black skirt and waded into the water up to her waist, but she could not get across the river. She shook her fist and shrieked at the girl. Nasta ran on.

When she arrived at the Sun's palace, she noticed that he had already found another maiden to take her place. The new girl was singing a happy song.

"Poor maiden, you have started singing too soon," Nasta warned the new girl.

When the Sun heard her speaking, he was very happy. He began hugging and kissing her, but she ran away from him and hid in a corner.

Then the Sun got very angry indeed. He put an evil spell on her, saying, "From this day forth you will no longer be called Nasta. Instead, you will be called Lasta the Swallow, and you will remain a swallow forever."

Nasta felt herself becoming smaller and smaller. She looked at her arms. They had turned into wings. She was a bird!

No one called her Nasta anymore. When she flew home to her village, the neighbors did not recognize her. They pointed at her and shouted, "Look, there's Lasta the Swallow, Lasta the Swallow!" Thus, the word *lasta* came to mean swallow in Slovenian.

The children of Nasta-Lasta were swallows, too, and that is how swallows came to live on earth. But never, not even once, did Nasta-Lasta regret her uncooperative behavior with the Sun. No matter what had happened to her, she had remained true to herself. Love cannot be forced. ✿

The Little Shepherd

(Croatia—Istria)

*O*nce upon a time in Istria, a little shepherd was grazing a herd of cows, a flock of sheep, and a few goats near the seashore.

It was afternoon, and the hot sun was beating down on the earth when the little shepherd came upon three beautiful girls sleeping in a green glen. They were *vilas*. (In the Balkans, fairies or nymphs with magical powers are called *vilas*.) They were indescribably beautiful and resembled one another so much that they looked like sisters. They lay quietly and were apparently sleeping very soundly.

The little shepherd did not give it a thought that they might be *vilas*. He assumed that they were ordinary girls who had lain down on the grass and had fallen asleep after becoming tired from strolling in the hot sun.

The sun will burn them, the boy thought. It's a pity for such pretty faces to be damaged. I must help them somehow.

He climbed a lime tree, broke off its leafy branches, and stuck them around the girls so that the sun's rays could not burn them anymore.

Soon afterward, the *vilas* awoke and got up. They pretended to be amazed and asked each other who had been so kind as to protect them from the sun's burning rays. Of course, they knew very well what had happened, for *vilas* never fall asleep. They just pretend to be sleeping. The *vilas* asked what had happened only in order to see whether the little shepherd would speak.

The little boy did not answer. He tried to run away because looking at the *vilas* hurt his eyes. The light from their glistening hair, which shone like gold, blinded him.

In an instant all three were beside him. He could not escape. They asked him what kind of reward he wanted for protecting them from the hot sun, but the boy dared not ask for anything.

They offered him a magic purse of money that would always be full of golden coins, but the little shepherd did not care at all about the magic purse. He was too young to know the value of money. Playing with the money and looking at it were boring. After all, he had cows and sheep that were dearer to him than anything else on earth. Why would he want money?

When the *vilas* discovered that the animals were dearest to the boy's heart, they said, "When you drive the herd home this evening, you will hear the ringing of bells coming from the direction of the sea. You will hear big bells with deep voices and little bells with high-pitched voices, but don't look back to see what is happening behind you until you reach home."

After giving the little shepherd these strange instructions, the girls disappeared. Because of their odd behavior, the boy realized that they were indeed *vilas*.

The sun sank slowly into the sea, and the little shepherd began driving his herd home. The closer he came to his house, the louder was the clanging and ringing behind his back. He began singing and picking flowers for his mother to distract himself from the ringing bells.

Soon he was thinking about how good his dinner would taste when he arrived home after a hard day's work. Finally, he forgot about the *vilas* and what they had told him.

When he was halfway home, he became so curious about the ringing of the bells that he turned around to see who could be behind him driving so many cattle home from pasture. No one in his village owned enough cattle to make such a great clamor of cowbells.

To his amazement he saw a large number of sheep, cows, and goats coming out of the sea, following his herd. The instant he turned around, they stopped coming out of the sea onto land. Only those that were already on dry land followed him home.

Had the little shepherd not turned around, he would have had an enormous number of new animals to add to his herd. However, he was not greedy for more than he already had. In fact, he was quite satisfied with the gift of the *vilas*.

He had enough animals so that he could give them to his poorer neighbors. From then on, no one in the village was needy anymore. The villagers prospered, and everyone remembered with gratitude the little shepherd's kindness. ❂

Tsar Dukljan

(Yugoslavia—Serbia)

Once upon a time Tsar Dukljan was hunting in the deep, dark forest when he came upon a lake. He crept close to the lake very quietly so that the wild animals would not notice his presence.

Having bent slightly over the lake, he was surprised to see a winged horse with a man on its back emerging from the water. The man had wings, too, and he had long, golden hair that hung down to the ground.

When the tsar saw the strange horse and rider, he hid behind a bush and began to peek out at them, watching to see what the man would do.

As soon as he came out onto dry land, the golden-haired man got off the horse and took out a long flute, spiraled and multicolored like a large snake, and began playing so badly that no one could bear to listen. All of nature seemed startled. Even the stones and trees began hissing in protest to the music.

The tsar was afraid of the strange man and his mysterious flute that caused even the stones to come alive. In his panic he drew an arrow on the man and wounded him severely through both wings.

The golden-haired man screamed out in pain so loudly that his cries could be heard as far as the heavens. "You may thank God that you saw me before I saw you," he shouted to Tsar Dukljan. "If I had seen you first, you'd have lived to regret it."

His threat struck fear into the tsar's heart. He ran up to the stranger with an unsheathed sword and was going to finish him off, but the man jumped into the lake in spite of his serious wound.

Tsar Dukljan grabbed the winged horse, mounted him, and started riding back to the palace as fast as he could. As soon as he mounted the horse and had traveled a short distance, a strange feeling came over him. He glanced over his shoulder and saw that he had sprouted wings. He was so startled that he jumped off the horse immediately. The minute that he touched the ground, his new wings disappeared. Because Tsar Dukljan was unaccustomed to seeing wings on himself, or on anyone else for that matter, he grabbed the horse by the reins and led him to the palace on foot.

Once he had arrived home, he told his family everything that had happened to him. His servants led the horse to the stables.

When the tsar's son, the tsarevich, heard about his father's adventures, he decided to set out for the lake himself without his father's knowledge. Everything happened according to the tsar's story. The tsarevich came upon the lake, but he did not creep up quietly as his father had done. Instead, he walked up to the lake boldly with a drawn arrow.

As he approached the water's edge, he noticed that a middle-aged woman was emerging from the lake. Her hair was unbraided, and she was wringing her hands and weeping inconsolably.

She walked onto the shore and looked at the tsar's son. When their eyes met, the tsarevich fainted on the spot, as if he had fallen dead.

The instant he fell, the winged horse back in his father's stables began shrieking and beating its wings. The great clamor and banging raised by the horse shook the entire palace.

Tsar Dukljan jumped up and ran down to the stables to see what was wrong.

"If you want to see your son alive," the horse said, "return me to the place from which I came."

The tsar was amazed that the horse could speak. He became frightened, just as he had earlier when he was confronted by the strange winged man who had the ability to make trees and stones come alive.

He decided that perhaps he should obey the horse's command, so he mounted bareback. The horse flew like lightning to the lake.

Tsar Dukljan saw his son stretched out, seemingly dead, beside the lake. A weeping woman was bending over him. When the tsar came closer, he froze in horror. The half-crazed woman was digging the eyes out of his son's head with a fish bone.

The tsar began wailing for his son.

"Let's forget the past," the horse shouted at the woman. "I'm back now, so let's exchange a son for a son and forgive the father."

The woman looked at the winged horse and obeyed him. She put the eyes back into the tsarevich's head and revived him with magic water from the lake, which she sprinkled onto his eyes. When he awoke, she gave him to the tsar.

"Now, give me the horse in return," she demanded.

The tsar returned the horse to the woman. Then he and his son hurried back to the palace, happy to have escaped alive.

For many days Tsar Dukljan pondered these mysterious events. "I'm back now, so let's exchange a son for a son and forgive the father," the horse had said. But the old woman had not exchanged a son for a son. Rather, she had exchanged a son for a horse.

Finally, the tsar decided that the horse must have been the son of the weeping woman and that the golden-haired man, whom he had wounded, must have been the horse's father. Never again did the tsar see the unusual family from the lake, nor did he care to see them. ❧

The Miser and the Generous Man

(Bosnia and Herzegovina)

There once lived a miser and a generous man. Together they set out to travel around the world with only fifty gold coins as their entire fortune. The good-hearted man had forty coins, and the miser had ten coins.

"Let's spend my forty coins first," the generous man said to the miser.

"Well, thanks, we'll do just that," the miser said, all too willing to agree.

After traveling for some time, they spent all of the generous man's money.

Then, the good-hearted man said to the miser, "Now let's spend your ten coins until we run into some good luck. Fortune is bound to come our way eventually."

However, the miser would not agree to share his fortune. "We spent your forty coins very quickly, and we'll spend my ten coins even faster," he answered. "Let's go our separate ways. You seek your fortune, and I'll seek mine."

They went on together for a short while. Then they came to a cross-road, and here they parted. The generous man went to the right, and the miser went to the left.

The good-hearted man traveled all day long. Toward evening he came to a town. No sooner had he entered the town than he began thinking of his plight. "What will I do in this town?" he asked aloud. "I don't have a cent to my name. What will I eat, and where will I sleep?"

Some old mills were located just outside of town. They had been abandoned forty years ago when the millstream had dried up. In desperation, the generous man went into one of these old mills to spend the night.

There was no place inside the mill to lie down, so he climbed behind the millstone and huddled there. At the stroke of midnight, he heard music, laughter, and singing. A merry troupe of devils entered the very same mill in which the good-hearted man was spending the night. Once inside the mill, they started playing the *gusle*, a one-stringed musical instrument, and singing merry songs.

When they had had their fill of playing and singing, the leader, who was also the oldest devil, said, "Stop! That's enough. Let's do something else now. Let's tell stories about the old days."

He began his story first. "Forty years ago, a river flowed on this spot, and grain used to be ground in these mills."

"If only the townspeople knew that there is a large stone blocking the spring that feeds the river and that the stone is located at the crossroad on the main street of town," the youngest devil said. "Then they would be able to repair the damage and have water again."

"Even greater wonders exist," added a third devil. "Do you remember that thieving barber who lives in the shop near the crossroad by the mosque, the one who cheats people by overcharging them? Well, there are seven kettles of gold coins in his shop. The coins once belonged to a tsar. Our ancestors stole them from the tsar and hid them there. If only the barber knew enough to lift a stone slab from the floor, the coins would appear. He wouldn't have to live in poverty anymore."

They talked until dawn about many other secrets. When it got light, the merry company disappeared. As soon as they had gone away, the generous man walked out of the mill and headed for town.

Once in town, he went into the local café. "Good people, why do you suffer from a lack of water?" he asked the townspeople gathered there.

"We have been suffering for forty years," the people answered.

"If you give me forty men, with God's help I'll be able to find the spring and dig it up," the generous man offered.

As soon as they heard that, the townspeople went to the vizier, a high official in the local government, to tell him what the stranger had said. The vizier was very happy. He summoned the good-hearted man and gave him not 40, but 100 men.

In addition, the vizier said to him, "If you find the spring, you will be well rewarded."

The townspeople followed the man to the crossroads on the main street of town. There, he began to dig. He ordered the men sent to help him to dig, too.

They began working. They dug and dug until they came to a stone. "There's no water here," they said. "It's no use digging!"

"Yes, there is water here. I'm certain of it," the generous man replied.

Again they began digging. They dug a trench around the stone. When they lifted the stone, water gushed out on all sides.

The people, who had been watching the proceedings, cheered, and they, too, began digging. Water began flowing as swiftly and abundantly as it had in the old days.

The vizier called the generous man before him to give him a reward. "What do you want as a reward?" the vizier asked. "How much money should I give you?"

"Honorable vizier," the generous man answered, "I ask only to be given the shop where the thieving barber lives."

The vizier commanded that the barber be called immediately. "Would you like to sell me your shop?" the vizier asked.

Now the barber was a very greedy man. He pondered over the vizier's words, then saw the opportunity to make a nice profit. "I would sell it for a good price," he replied.

The vizier bought the shop for the good-hearted man and presented him with a handsome white stallion as well.

As soon as the generous man left the vizier's mansion, he set out for his new shop. He immediately covered the windows with blankets, lit a candle, and began searching for the gold coins that were hidden there.

After digging under the stone slab for a while, he dug up a kettle full of coins. Then, he dug and dug some more until he found six more kettles. He took several chests and poured the coins into them, then nailed them shut.

Soon after, the good-hearted man built a modest little home and got married. He purchased several shops and became a prosperous merchant, respected and loved by the townspeople.

One morning while sitting in his shop, he noticed a poor man with clothes all tattered and torn. As soon as he saw him, he recognized him as his old friend, the miser. He invited him into his shop and offered him a seat. In the evening, he took him to his home to spend the night and showed him his wealth.

Seeing so much wealth, the miser was overcome with awe. After recovering from his surprise, he asked, "In God's name, brother, where did you get so much money?"

"Didn't I tell you that we'd run into good luck?" the generous man replied. He told his friend everything he had heard at the mill and everything that had happened to him since that lucky day.

Then the miser said to the good-hearted man, "You can have your old coins. Who cares about them? Just take me to the mill where you spent the night."

The generous man took him to the mill and showed him where he had slept when he spent the night there. The miser lay down on the same spot, and the generous man returned home.

Everything happened exactly the way it had when the good-hearted man had spent the night there. When it was midnight, the devils came by. When they entered the mill, they began playing and singing.

After they had played and sung to their hearts' content, the oldest devil stood up and said, "We've had enough playing and singing. Let's tell some stories about the old days."

"How can I tell about the old days?" asked the youngest devil. "When we told stories before, water started flowing again out of the spring that feeds the river and the gold coins were discovered. Someone must have been listening to us while we were telling stories."

"Then let's search the mill first to see if someone is here," another devil proposed.

"Good idea!" shouted his friends. They got up and searched every nook and cranny until they found the miser.

The miser begged for mercy to no avail. The devils were so angry that they grabbed hold of him and tore him to shreds.

That is how the miser ended his miser's life, but the generous man lived honestly and happily with his wealth until he was a very old man. ❈

A Copper Coin or Your Head

(Yugoslavia—Montenegro)

The section of Yugoslavia called Montenegro, whose name means Black Mountains, is rugged and mountainous. A fiercely independent people have always lived there.

When the Ottoman Turks invaded the southern Balkans, they were able to conquer Bosnia, Herzegovina, and even Serbia, which was defeated in the Battle of Kosovo in 1389. The Montenegrins, however, resisted the Turks passionately and were never totally subdued. They always enjoyed a degree of freedom that their South Slavic brothers in surrounding areas lacked.

Typically, Montenegrin fighters would attack the Turks, then hide deep in the mountains where they could not be found. There is a legend that reveals the spirit of these brave people. It goes like this:

At the beginning of the eighteenth century, Grand Vizier Ćuprilić and his army pillaged Montenegro. The Grand Vizier, who represented the Ottoman Turks, went to the Bjelice area to extract a tribute from the people.

Beforehand, he sent a messenger to the local *vojvoda*, or governor, Vukota Mrvaljević, with an order for the *vojvoda* to pay the Grand Vizier a tax of just one single copper coin in the name of the people of Bjelice. The Grand Vizier considered that the tax was not so high as to cause the Montenegrins too much humiliation, yet it would remind them that the Turks were their masters.

"The people of Bjelice have never given tribute either to the Emperor or to Caesar, and they aren't going to pay now," said Vukota Mrvaljević.

The messenger delivered Vukota's reply to the vizier. Vukota, knowing the fate that awaited him, fled with his people into the mountains to a cave near the village of Stavor.

The Turks surrounded the cave and captured Vukota alive. Moreover, they took his two sons prisoner and led the young men out to be executed right there in front of their father. They intended to kill Vukota, too, for his disobedience.

"Oh, Father, what do they intend to do to us?" asked the worried younger son.

"Never mind, son. Our execution will be over quickly, but the satisfaction we get from not giving the Turks the copper coin they demanded will long be remembered. Our deed will live on forever and never be forgotten."

And so it came to pass. The legend of the copper coin and the bravery of the father who was ready to sacrifice his own life and the lives of his sons in the name of freedom has been told and retold, and is told to this very day. ✿

Beautiful Mara

(Macedonia)

*O*nce upon a time there lived a man and his wife, and they had a daughter called Beautiful Mara. One day when she was almost sixteen years old, the girl took her embroidery frame and some silken threads and went into the garden to embroider under the cool shade of a tree.

After a while, a bird perched on a branch above her head began singing. "Beautiful Mara, you will marry a dead man," it sang dismally. Mara burst into tears when she heard the bird's cruel prediction and went into the house. Her mother was surprised that the girl had returned so quickly from the garden. Mara told her what the bird had said.

"Oh, daughter, you are your mother's only child. Do you really think that we would give you to someone from the Kingdom of the Dead?" her mother reasoned with her.

For three days the bird repeated its song. The mother had to comfort her distraught daughter constantly, assuring her that nothing so terrible would ever happen.

That was all very well, but the next year twelve men from an unknown land came to visit them. The twelve men were matchmakers, who had come to arrange a marriage. "On behalf of our friend, who couldn't accompany us, we have come to ask for Beautiful Mara's hand in marriage," they said to the girl's parents.

It was as if the lips of Mara's mother and father had turned to stone, for they did not refuse. They agreed to give her to the strange man they had never met who lived in an unknown kingdom they had never seen.

The twelve matchmakers said, "Mara must come with us right now."

The girl was dumbfounded. It was as if her parents were under a spell. They agreed to let her go without even asking the name of the bridegroom despite their previous assurances that they would save her from the terrible fate of marrying a dead man.

The twelve strangers set out quickly with Mara, who was still in a daze, unable to believe what had happened. On and on they traveled, and finally they arrived at a barren, black mountain whose craggy peak was in sharp contrast to the blue sky.

They came to an opening in a boulder on the mountainside, and six men led Beautiful Mara into the mountain. The remaining six men followed her so that she had six men in front of her and six men behind her. There was no escape.

Soon they found themselves in another land. They came to a pretty little cottage with a garden.

"Beautiful Mara," the matchmakers said, "this is the Kingdom of the Dead. Our friend saw you embroidering in the garden one day and fell in love with you. We brought you to this cottage as he asked. Your bridegroom will arrive this evening. Right now he's away at work."

Soon Mara became accustomed to her surroundings and felt better. She had expected the Kingdom of the Dead to be an ugly, bleak place, but the cottage was clean and pleasant enough.

When it grew dark, she found herself in a strange, silent world, a place without people. The absence of other human beings bothered her.

Finally, when it was pitch black, her husband arrived. Because of the darkness, Mara could not see him.

He greeted her and said, "You will be my wife, and I will be your husband. We'll be very happy together. I am going to set only one condition, and it is very important that you fulfill it faithfully. You must never turn on a light—neither a lamp nor a torch—nor may you light a fire during our life together. Dinner and supper will be sent to you already prepared so that you will have no need to kindle a fire.

"I leave early in the morning for work and return late in the evening. Please obey my request, for if you don't do what I have asked, I will disappear, never to return. Then you'll never find me unless you put on a pair of iron shoes and take an iron staff and travel around the world searching for me."

Mara grew to love her husband dearly. Although she could not see him, she could listen to his gentle voice, and he was always good to her. They lived in happiness for four or five months. Then one evening, Mara turned to her husband and said, "I would like to go see my mother and father."

After a moment of silence, her husband said, "Tomorrow I will send for my twelve friends to take you home to your parents. Stay with them for a couple of days, and my friends will return to take you back here."

The next day Mara went to visit her mother and father. They welcomed her warmly. "Where have you come from so unexpectedly?" they asked. "We have been worried about you ever since the day we gave you away in marriage. We have always remembered how the bird told you that you would marry a dead man."

"And so it was, Mother, but I love him. I like it there in the Kingdom of the Dead. Food and drink, everything is brought to me already prepared. Late at night my husband returns from work. He leaves early in the morning, so I don't know what he looks like. But he is kind to me."

Mara's mother was not satisfied. "Oh, daughter, isn't it hard to live with someone you've never seen? What if your husband is an ugly monster? Would you still love him? When you return, take three candles with you. Light them at midnight when your husband is asleep. Then you will see what kind of man he is."

Mara didn't know what to do. Should she obey her husband or take her mother's advice? He never forbade me to light candles, the young woman mused. He mentioned lamps and fires and torches but not candles.

The two days passed quickly, and the twelve friends came to accompany Beautiful Mara home. With her she took the three candles that her mother had given her.

She arrived at her cottage and found everything ready, dinner and supper. When night fell, her husband came home. He was very happy to have her back. After they had eaten supper and talked for a while, he lay down and fell asleep.

Mara could not resist the temptation to see what kind of man she had married. At midnight she lit one of the candles. When she saw that her husband was not a monster, but a handsome young man, she was happy.

She lit a second candle, then a third candle so that she could have a better look, but suddenly a drop of wax from the third candle dripped onto her husband's face. He let out a terrifying scream of pain and jumped up in despair.

"Oh, Mara, why have you betrayed me?" he cried. "Now you will never see me again!" And suddenly he disappeared.

Mara waited the next evening and the evening after, but her husband did not return. A month passed, then two, then three, but he never came. Her meals, dinner and supper, arrived regularly.

Now and then her husband's friends, who had brought her to the cottage, appeared and asked her if she needed anything. She always said one and the same thing to them. "Please find me a pair of iron shoes and an iron staff."

One day they brought the iron shoes and the iron staff that she had requested. Mara put on the shoes, took the staff in her hand, and set out on a long journey to find her beloved husband.

For many days she crossed mountains and rivers and valleys until her feet ached. She searched in caves and in forests and in cities, but she found her husband nowhere. Eventually, her iron shoes became so worn that her toes were exposed, and the staff was worn too short for her to lean on.

One evening when she was spending the night in a cave, she gave birth to a little son. She stared and stared at him because the little boy resembled his father very much. The next day she wrapped him in swaddling clothes and went on her way in search of his father.

Finally, when she was very tired from having walked so far, she came to a fountain. The fountain had two openings. From one opening, milk was flowing and from the other honey was flowing.

This fountain belonged to the sisters of Mara's husband. There were three of them. Beautiful Mara did not even know that her husband had sisters; he had never mentioned them.

It was customary for the oldest girl to come to the fountain in the morning. At noon the middle girl always came, and the youngest one would come in the evening.

Mara sat near the fountain to rest. That morning her husband's oldest sister came. "Please give us a little something to drink," Mara said to her. "If you have no pity for me, then take pity on this baby boy I'm holding in my arms."

The oldest sister did not even glance at her. Nor did she give her anything to drink. She poured out some milk and honey for herself and went away.

At midday the middle sister came. Again Mara spoke. "I've come a long way. If you have no pity for me, then take pity on this baby boy. My lips are burning. Please give us something to drink."

This sister did not look at her either. She poured out milk and honey for herself and went away.

Toward evening the youngest sister came. Mara began begging while she was still far away. "Two girls who looked like you came in the morning and at noon, but they wouldn't give us anything to drink. I'm not asking for myself, but for the sake of my little baby. We have traveled a long way, and we're very tired. Please give me a little milk to moisten his lips."

The youngest sister was kinder than the others. She poured some milk and honey into a cup and gave it to Mara to drink. When she looked at the child, she was startled because she saw that he looked like her brother. She filled her jug quickly and went home.

When darkness fell, the three girls and their brother, Mara's husband, gathered to eat supper.

"Sister, why don't you eat your supper? Are you sick or perhaps angry?" the brother asked his youngest sister.

"I'm neither sick, nor angry, brother. But a beggar woman is sitting beside our fountain with a baby boy in her arms. I feel sorry for her. She is wearing iron shoes, and she walks with an iron staff. Her baby, dear brother, looks just like you. They have traveled a long way, and they're hungry and tired. Until we invite them to our table to share our meal, I cannot sit down."

When the brother heard his sister's words, he knew that the woman must be his wife, their sister-in-law. He explained what had happened.

"Mara promised that she would never turn on a light, but she broke her word. She lit three candles that hurt my eyes and almost blinded me, so I left her and came to you. Because she broke her promise, my wife had to put on iron shoes and take an iron staff in her hands. I see that she has suffered very much and has done everything as I told her. Go, bring her here. Let's forget the past and begin anew."

All three girls hurried to the fountain. They brought their sister-in-law and her baby into their home. The happy husband was overjoyed to be reunited with his beautiful wife, and he was delighted with his new little son.

They lived happily ever after in the Kingdom of the Dead, and no one ever, ever turned on a light or lit a fire of any kind again. ❁

COLOR PHOTOGRAPHS

The photographs represent the traditional Balkans. Because they were taken shortly after World War II, almost 50 years ago, they represent the region before it was industrialized. They reflect diverse cultural settings and show how the people of the Balkans encountered each other in multi-ethnic market places.

Serbian woman and child in Bosnia.
Photograph by Joel M. Halpern.

Little Bosnian girl.
Photograph by Joel M. Halpern.

Muslim men socialize in a mosque courtyard. The white band indicates its wearer has been on a pilgrimage to Mecca.

Photography by Joel M. Halpern.

Twin girls from Serbia spinning flax and displaying chandeliers they made in celebration of the coming of electrification.

Photograph by Joel M. Halpern.

Romany (Gypsy) drummer and Macedonian dancers in Macedonia.

Photograph by Joel M. Halpern.

Boy playing flute at the Maglaj market.
Photograph by Joel M. Halpern.

Baker on a sidestreet in Sarajevo, Bosnia.
Photograph by Joel M. Halpern.

**An Albanian from Kosovo in a skullcap and a Serb in a fur hat
chat at the Maglaj Bosnian cattle market.**
Photograph by Joel M. Halpern.

Muslim women plowing.
Photograph by Joel M. Halpern.

Washday is a social event in Macedonia.
Photograph by Joel M. Halpern.

Fish nets drying in the sun near Ohrid, Macedonia.
Photograph by Joel M. Halpern.

Slovenian barn with corn drying.
Photograph by Joel M. Halpern.

Bosnian man using a wooden plow.
Photograph by Joel M. Halpern.

Modest couple outside home in Serbia with grapes drying beneath the eaves.
Photograph by Joel M. Halpern.

Albanian man and woman chatting at the Peč market.

Photograph by Joel M. Halpern.

A Muslim rope seller and his Croat customer at the Maglaj market.

Photograph by Joel M. Halpern.

Muslim homes near Sarajevo. Steep roofs shed snow.
Photograph by Joel M. Halpern.

Thatching a roof.
Photograph by Joel M. Halpern.

Wedding party outside church.
Photograph by Joel M. Halpern.

Serbian winter grave ritual honoring the dead with a feast.
Photograph by Joel M. Halpern.

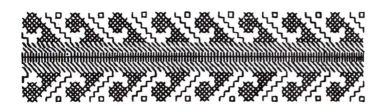

Part II

ANIMAL TALES

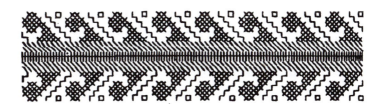

The Ox and the Mouse

(Bosnia and Herzegovina)

An ox was lying in the stable chewing his cud when a little mouse came out of the wall and began strutting and jumping with a carefree air on the ox's back. The ox heard the commotion and gave the mouse a dirty look.

"Isn't there enough space in this stable?" he asked. "Why do you have to play on my back? Perhaps you don't know who I am."

"Oh, yes, I know who you are," said the mouse. "You're an ox. You are big and strong, but good and kind. If I walk on your back, it won't do you any harm. And, besides, I like your soft, warm fur." The mouse gave a little leap of joy and slid all the way down the ox's furry back.

"Just because I'm good and kind doesn't mean I'll stand for any old mouse to strut and jump on my kindness. Now scram, pest! I have only to flick my tail to toss you up to the top of the stable and through the roof."

"Please don't do that, Mr. Ox. I know that you could do it if you wanted to. But since you are good and kind to everyone else, be kind to me, too. Maybe the time will come when I can be of use to you."

"Thousands of nincompoops like you can neither harm nor help me. I'm neither afraid of you, nor do I expect that the likes of you will ever be of any help to me. Get out of here before I smash you!" bellowed the ox.

The mouse quickly jumped off the ox's back and crawled into a hole in the wall.

Several days later, the same ox was in the stable tied to a post near the manger. Somehow he had managed to wrap the rope around his neck. The tangled rope was choking him. He began jumping up and down in pain and breathing through his nostrils so heavily and raspingly that the mouse heard the commotion. She came running.

"What's happened to you?" she asked.

"Something terrible. As you see, I'm strangling myself."

"Butt with your horns and tear the rope off."

"I would if the rope wasn't around my neck. Please help me. If you don't, I'm sure to die."

"I would like to help you, but I don't dare jump onto your neck. Remember what you told me a few days ago?"

"Never mind that now. You can jump on my neck and even on my eyes, but please help me."

The mouse jumped onto ox's neck and worked with all her might. Little by little she gnawed the rope until it broke and was just barely able to save the ox's life.

When the ox caught his breath, he was sorry that he had spoken harshly to the little mouse. He was ashamed of himself for having made fun of the possibility that someday the mouse might help him.

"Anyone who abuses his power by hurting someone, as I did, deserves to be hated," he said, "but please don't hate me, little mouse. Forgive me for being so mean to you, and let's be friends."

From that day on, the ox and the mouse were the dearest of friends. ❁

The Bear, the Pig, and the Fox

(Yugoslavia—Serbia)

A bear, a pig, and a fox became friends. They agreed that together they would plow the earth and plant some wheat so that they would have enough to eat when winter came. They talked about dividing the work equally and about finding some grain to plant.

The pig said, "I'll go into the shed and get some grain. Because my nose is especially made for digging and routing, I'll plow the soil with my snout."

The bear said, "I'll plant the wheat."

And the fox said, "I'll break up the large clumps of soil with my tail."

Each one did his job as agreed. They plowed and planted. When the harvest came, they talked about how they would harvest the grain.

The pig said, "I'll gather it."

The bear said, "I'll bind it into sheaves."

The fox said, "I'll collect the sheaves."

Everything went smoothly. They harvested the grain and bound it into sheaves. Then they began to discuss how they would thresh the wheat.

The pig said, "I'll make the threshing floor."

The bear said, "I'll carry the sheaves to the threshing floor, and I'll thresh them."

The pig said, "I'll shake the sheaves to separate the straw from the wheat."

The fox said, "I'll separate the chaff from the grain with my tail."

The pig said, "I'll sift through the wheat and remove any dirt that may have gotten mixed in with the grain."

And the bear said, "I'll divide up the grain."

The pig sifted through the grain as she had agreed. The bear divided the grain, but he did not divide it equally. He gave only straw to the pig, and he took all the wheat for himself. The pig did not mind this arrangement because she needed the straw to make a nice, soft bed for herself in her pigsty.

To the fox, the bear gave nothing. When the fox appealed to the pig to help reason with the bear, the pig refused. Then the fox got angry and decided to go to the tsar, the country's ruler, to bring charges against the bear and the pig. She told them that she would be bringing back one of the tsar's deputies and that the deputy, who had no patience with rascals, would see to it that the grain was divided fairly.

After the fox had disappeared down the road, the pig and the bear got scared. "She really means business," the bear said to the pig. "Let's hide. Bury yourself in the straw, pig, and I'll climb up this pear tree."

The pig burrowed into the straw, and the bear went up the tree.

Meanwhile, the fox never made it to the tsar's palace. As she was walking down the road, she met a cat. The cat was a charmer with a sleek coat of fur and nice manners, so the fox liked him right away. She asked the cat to be her friend. Then the fox told him that she knew of a wonderful place where there were hundreds of mice.

"Where, my friend?" asked the cat with interest.

"Just follow me, and I'll take you to the threshing floor that the pig built. You can catch some nice fat mice there."

The cat, knowing that there were always plenty of mice under a threshing floor, followed willingly. On the way he chased birds playfully, running first up the trees beside the road, then scrambling down into the ditch.

The bear was observing the cat from his seat in the pear tree while he was still far away. "Bad news, pig! It's the fox," the bear said. "She's bringing a mean-looking deputy with her. The old fool's covered from head to toe with mink, and he's wild with rage. He's so angry that he's running all over the road catching every bird he can get his hands on. We're in for trouble now!"

Then the cat disappeared from sight. Before the bear and the pig could count to three, the cat was creeping through the grass toward the threshing floor. While searching for mice, he began to poke through the straw.

The pig was sitting in the pile of straw wondering all the while what the terrible deputy looked like. Curiosity finally got the best of her, and she raised her head to see what was going on.

The cat, thinking that the pig's snout was a mouse, gave a leap and grabbed the pig by the nose with his claws.

"Oink, o-o-oink!" the frightened pig squealed in pain as she jumped up and ran to the brook to stick her injured snout into the cool water.

The pig's sudden appearance frightened the cat, who had been expecting a mouse. He scrambled up the pear tree.

The distraught bear assumed that the cat had passed judgment on the pig and had executed her and that now the cat was coming up the tree after him. The bear became so rattled that he fell—kerplop—out of the pear tree onto the ground.

As soon as he could scramble to his feet, he ran to the forest like a streak of lightning, despite his heavy layers of jiggling fat. He was never seen again.

The happy fox was left with all the grain and the straw as well. Most important of all, she had found a new friend. ❀

The Horse and the Wolf

(Bosnia and Herzegovina)

*O*nce upon a time there was a wolf that was despised by every shepherd for miles around because he was always trying to steal lambs from their flocks for his dinner. After several years had passed, the wolf became old and got tired of being chased by people, so he renounced his sins and set out on a pilgrimage to the Holy City of Mecca.

On the way, he met a ram. "Where are you headed, dear friend?" the wolf asked him.

"Oh, I'm running away from my master because I heard that he intends to slaughter me tomorrow."

"Then come along with me," the wolf said.

"But you might try to eat me for dinner," the ram protested.

"Oh, no," the wolf replied. "I got tired of being chased by people, so I renounced my sins, and I'm going on a pilgrimage to the Holy City of Mecca."

The ram agreed to accompany the wolf, and they continued the journey together.

After a short time had passed, they met a fox. "What happened to you that made you decide to go on a journey?" asked the wolf.

"I got tired of being chased by people for attacking their chickens, so I've set out to search for better luck," the fox answered.

"Come with us to the Holy City of Mecca," the wolf proposed.

The fox liked the idea very much, so she went with them. The three friends walked along together until they met a scraggly old horse.

"What misfortune has befallen you?" the wolf asked. "Why have you decided to go on a journey?"

"Oh, leave me alone, for goodness sake! My life has been filled with hard work and sadness. I served my master faithfully for many years. Every day I went to the forest for wood and I carried heavy sacks of grain to the mill and back home again. And now that I have become old and weak, my master has decided to kill me so that he can make a profit by selling my hide. Now I am running I know not where to save myself from being killed." Then the sad horse asked them where they were traveling to and what misfortune had befallen them.

Each animal told of his bad luck. They said that they were going on a pilgrimage to the Holy City of Mecca, and they invited the horse along. He agreed willingly, and they set out.

They went along quite happily until the wolf ordered them to stop to rest. After they had rested, the wolf felt hungry.

"I've become very hungry," he said to his newly made friends. "I simply can't take another step until I've had something to eat. Tell me, which one of you shall I eat first?"

"I'm very young, as you see," said the ram. "It would be a pity for you to eat me."

"I'm too small," the fox said. "You wouldn't get enough of me. But the horse is old and has lived long enough. And what's more, you would have so much to eat that there would be enough left over for me, too."

The horse got angry at the wolf for betraying their friendship by deciding to eat one of them. He was angry at the fox, too, for telling the wolf to eat him up.

"Do you know how to read?" he asked the fox.

"No, I don't," the fox replied. "But the wolf is a very intelligent animal, and he reads very well."

"All right, then. Before you kill me, wolf, please read what my master has branded on the shoe of my right hind hoof," begged the horse.

The wolf decided to oblige the horse by granting his dying wish. He went over to the hoof.

Then the horse raised his right hind leg. Just as the wolf began reading the words forged on the shoe, the horse hit him in the head so hard that the wolf was immediately stretched out on the ground with his legs jerking in the air.

When the fox saw this, she began skipping around the wolf playfully. "Oh boy, joy of joys, the wolf is dead," she cried.

Then the animals went their separate ways. How they fared in life, nobody knows, but the wolf paid for his treachery with his head. ✿

The Mouse and the Ant

(Yugoslavia—Kosovo and Metohija)

A mouse asked an ant if he could borrow some wheat from her. The ant lent him the grain gladly, but then the ant did not have enough grain for herself. She asked the mouse to give back some of the wheat.

"Please give me back some of the wheat I lent you, mouse," said the ant, "because I don't have anything to eat, myself."

"I don't have it to give you," the mouse squeaked. "I ate it all up." The mouse was lying, of course. He planned to cheat the ant out of her grain, and he did not care if she starved to death.

The ant waited a few days until she became so thin she was hardly bigger than a speck of dust. Once again she asked for some grain, but the mouse refused to give it back.

"Give it to me, or I'll bring charges against you," the ant threatened.

"Do whatever you want. I simply don't have it to give you."

The two animals went to court. The cat, the tsar of the mice, stood in judgment over them in court.

The ant went up to the cat and said, "The mouse won't return the wheat I gave him. What should I do?"

"Go ask him once more," advised the cat. "If he won't give it to you, then we'll arrest him."

The ant went up to the mouse. "Will you give me the wheat I loaned you? If you don't, I'll bring charges against you."

The mouse still refused to return the grain.

Meanwhile, the cat went behind a curtain. She listened to the proceedings.

"Will you give me back some of the wheat that I loaned you?" the ant asked again.

"I don't have it!" the mouse replied stubbornly.

"Meow-w-w!" cried the cat, still hidden behind the curtain.

"What's that noise? Who is it?" asked the mouse.

The cat's "meow" sounded like a lion's roar to the little mouse, which thought that a lion had come to force him to give back the grain.

"Have you come for me?" asked the mouse.

The cat is a very stern judge. He might just as well be a lion, so fierce is he. "Give me a sack of grain right now!" the cat demanded, and he leapt onto the mouse. Greed always leads to grief. ❀

The Short Tail

(Croatia—Istria)

Once upon a time there was a rabbit that had a short tail. If his tail had been longer, my tale would have been, too. ✹

The Little Hedgehog

(Slovenia)

A woman was kneading dough to make bread. Jánček, her son, was pestering her as usual because he wanted to help with the kneading.

"Go away, little hedgehog!" his mother cried in annoyance. She always called Jánček "little hedgehog" when she was angry or impatient with him.

Jánček and his mother lived many years ago when more miracles took place than take place today. So, no sooner had the mother called her son "little hedgehog" than the boy changed into an honest-to-goodness hedgehog.

There was no proper place for a hedgehog in the house, so Jánček left home and went into the forest. There, beneath the hollow of a pear tree, he dug a hole and lived in it for seven years.

Beyond the forest was a count's castle. One day the count went hunting and got lost in the woods. He searched for the road for a long time, but he could not find it. Finally, he became very tired, and he sat down right beneath the pear tree.

While the count was resting beneath the tree, Jánček the Hedgehog started whistling happily.

"Why are you whistling, hedgehog?" asked the count. "Why are you so happy?"

"I'm happy," Janček the Hedgehog answered, "because I know very well that you can't get out of the forest without my help."

The count became hopeful. "Do you know the way out of the forest?"

"Of course. I'll accompany you to your castle if you pay me well, Count."

"What do you want in payment for your services?"

"Give me one of your daughters in marriage."

They stood bargaining for a long time. Finally, the count had to consent to the price; otherwise he would never get out of the deep forest.

The hedgehog showed him the way out and accompanied the count directly to his castle.

Early the next morning, whistling a merry tune, Janček the Hedgehog returned to the count's home. He had come to pay a visit. "Good morning, good morning!" shouted Janček. "I've come for my pay. Give me one of your daughters."

The count had already given orders to his three daughters concerning how they should behave if the hedgehog came. They closed the castle doors quickly, opened the windows, and watched to see what the poor hedgehog would do.

A big rooster was strutting about the count's courtyard. Janček the Hedgehog saw him, and with a hop he leaped onto his back.

The rooster was frightened. "Erk! Erk!" he squawked, and he flew onto the windowsill with the hedgehog on his back. The count's daughters jumped away from the window in surprise.

"Hello, ladies," the hedgehog called out boldly. "Decide quickly which one of you will marry me."

"I wouldn't marry a count, let alone a hedgehog!" the oldest daughter announced disdainfully.

"I'm waiting for a king to come along to marry me," said the middle daughter, and she burst out laughing at the funny-looking hedgehog.

"I will marry you because you saved my father's life," the youngest girl said quietly.

Her sisters looked at her in horror. Who in their right mind would want to marry an ugly hedgehog?

The count tried to dissuade his daughter, but it was no use.

"I must marry the hedgehog, Father, because you gave your word. It's wrong to break a promise, and I won't let you do so for my sake."

Finally, the count reluctantly agreed to the marriage. He had the horses harnessed to his best carriage, and he ordered the wedding guests to assemble in the church. The youngest daughter sat down in the carriage. She took Janček the Hedgehog on her lap, and they drove off to the wedding ceremony.

The sisters followed in another carriage. Laughing all the way to church, they mocked their younger sister and her husband-to-be. "Her hedgehog will teach her how to hunt for food at night," one sister said.

"Yes," the other chimed in. "They'll dine on snakes and birds' eggs." The two girls broke into giggles.

The wedding party entered the church. With tears in her eyes, the youngest sister approached the church altar holding the hedgehog, which was seated on a silk pillow.

As they stepped in front of the altar, something wonderful happened. Janček the Hedgehog shed his skin and changed into a handsome young man right before the eyes of the wedding guests.

When the sisters saw the splendid youth, envy gnawed at their hearts like a green worm.

"You are too young to get married. Let me have him," said the middle sister to the young bride.

"No, no, I accept him, myself. You can't have him because you are only a child," the oldest sister protested.

J\v{c}ek embraced his little bride happily and said, "Because you agreed to marry me, the spell that my mother accidentally placed on me has been lifted. Now I will never have to wear the hedgehog skin again. I will marry you and no one else."

The two sisters began to pout, but no one paid any attention to them. The wedding took place as planned, and there was a great feast afterward. ✿

Bey Zlatum

(Bosnia and Herzegovina)

Once upon a time there was a poor man who had neither house nor property. He expected death to come any day, and he was just barely able to exist living beneath two planks of wood thrown together at the side of the road.

He had a shed in which he stored some meal in a secret place. As luck would have it, a fox began visiting his shed. She visited his meal bin every day until one day he caught sight of her and began lying in wait to see if he could catch her with his bare hands. He was so poor that he was unable to buy a gun or even a lock for his door to keep the fox out.

Day after day went by, but the fox always got away. The poor man was not able to get close enough to the fox to lay a hand on her.

Watching her attack his supply of meal, which decreased each night, he finally determined to find a way to make a lock for the door. Before he had to go to all that trouble, however, his luck changed.

One morning when he got out of bed, the fox was strolling leisurely around his storage shed, and he had an opportunity to catch her. This time the fox did not notice his presence. The poor man went inside and grabbed her.

He carried the fox outside and tied her up. Then he went to get a stick because he did not have an ax. He wanted to kill her so that she would never be able to return to steal his meal again.

When the fox saw that she was about to lose her life, she began to beg. "Please let me go! If you do, I'll see to it that you marry the tsar's daughter."

The man felt sorry for the fox. His idea to kill her had seemed foolish from the beginning, but he was driven to such a desperate act because she had intended to cheat him out of all his meal.

If I kill her, it will be of no benefit to me, he thought to himself. But if I let her go, she'll have learned a lesson. She won't dare come here again. I think I'll let her go.

He untied her. As soon as she was free, the fox lit out for the woods.

"Where are you going, fox?" the poor man asked, noting that she seemed to have no intention of thanking him.

She turned to him. "I'm going to the tsar to ask for the hand of his daughter, the tsarevna, in marriage for you."

"Never mind, Auntie Fox," he said. "Even if you could manage to get the tsar to agree to it, I don't have a decent home to bring the tsarevna to."

The fox waved her tail and said, "That's not your worry." Then she ran off into the forest.

She set out for the tsar's palace and arrived there safely. Once there, she greeted the first guard she met. "May God help us!" she said to him.

"God be with you, Auntie Fox," the guard replied.

"May I see the honorable tsar?" she asked.

"Wait here, Auntie Fox, and I'll ask."

The guard went to the tsar and told him that the fox had come on business and that she had asked if she could see the tsar about a very important matter.

The tsar said that he would grant her an audience, so the guard told Auntie Fox that she could go in to see the tsar.

Auntie immediately went before the tsar and said, "May God help us, honorable tsar!"

"God be with you, Auntie Fox," answered the tsar. "What misfortune brings you to me?"

"Honorable tsar, it's not a question of misfortune. I have something to tell you, if you will allow me."

"You know, Auntie, that one may speak freely before my throne and ask for anything," answered the tsar. "So, if you have something to say, speak up."

The fox needed no more encouragement. She was as eager to speak as a bully is to quarrel.

"Honorable tsar," she began, "I have heard that you have a daughter whose beauty is rumored about the world. I have a young man by the name of Bey Zlatum. He is a fine, rich gentleman. Everyone says so. He's 109 times better looking than your daughter. I'm telling you the truth. Now, I ask you, do you want to give your daughter in marriage to my Bey Zlatum?"

"How can I give her when I don't know if the girl is in agreement?" the tsar answered. "I won't give her against her will because, after all, she is my daughter, and I love her."

"Let me ask her," said Auntie Fox. "We'll see what she has to say."

The tsar ordered his daughter to come to the throne room. As soon as she appeared, the tsar told her everything. Then he said, "My dear child, if you wish to marry Bey Zlatum, just say so. If you don't want to marry him, tell Auntie Fox, and she'll go away."

The tsar's daughter listened, then lowered her eyes and was silent.

The fox started to run out the door, acting as if she was leaving because of a terrible insult. "I swear on my favorite chicken coop," she said, "that my Bey Zlatum is 109 times better looking than you and 10 times richer than your father. Don't give it another thought. Just give your promise, and you won't regret it."

When the beautiful tsarevna saw that her father was not against it, she gave her promise. Then she went out into the garden to take a stroll while she made plans for the wedding.

The tsar turned to Auntie Fox. "Look, Auntie Fox, you heard what she said. Now you have only to take her to Bey Zlatum's mansion. But don't come to get her until half a year has passed. She won't be ready sooner, because everyone in the palace will be busy sewing a splendid wardrobe for her and preparing for the wedding day. Don't bring less than 500 guests to the wedding. The more, the merrier."

As soon as the fox heard the tsar's words, she left and hurried back to her Bey Zlatum.

When she arrived, Bey Zlatum was very happy because he did not think he would ever see Auntie Fox again. But he was worried when she told him that she had asked for the hand of the tsar's daughter in marriage and that after half a year had passed he and 500 wedding guests were to fetch the tsarevna and bring her to his humble home.

"What will we do, Auntie?" Bey Zlatum asked. "God is our only hope. As you see, I don't have a thing to my name, much less am I able to meet royalty and bring the tsar's daughter home."

"Don't worry about anything," answered Auntie Fox. "I'll arrange it all."

Day after day passed. As the time when they would have to go to the tsar's palace drew near, Auntie Fox did not even think about the wedding procession, but her Bey Zlatum racked his brains trying to think of a solution to their dilemma

When the appointed day came, Auntie Fox said, "Let's go, Bey Zlatum!"

"Where are our guests? Where is my wedding robe?" he asked.

"Don't worry about it," replied Auntie Fox. "Just follow me."

Bey Zlatum, already knowing what would come of it, took his fate into his hands and followed Auntie Fox.

As they approached the tsar's palace, Bey Zlatum again asked, "For goodness sake, what will we do, Auntie?"

Once again Auntie Fox answered, "Don't worry about anything."

Not far from the tsar's palace, they came upon a mud puddle. As soon as Auntie Fox caught sight of the puddle, she began to roll in it. She told Bey Zlatum to do the same. Because he had obeyed Auntie in everything else so far, he obeyed her in this, too, and he began rolling in the mud.

If only you had seen what they looked like when they came out of the mud! Auntie Fox could barely drag her mud-caked tail, and Bey Zlatum kept breaking clumps of soil off his body to make it easier to move as he walked down the road. Finally, they arrived at the tsar's palace.

Auntie Fox went up to the guards, for she had learned long ago that one must always walk through the main entrance. She ordered them to ask the tsar if Auntie Fox and Bey Zlatum might come before him.

The guards went to their commander and requested that he send the fastest among them to the tsar to ask about Auntie's business, because Auntie Fox wanted to finish it up as soon as possible.

The commander, when he heard that Auntie Fox was in a hurry, summoned his grandfather from guard duty and commanded him to run quickly to the tsar on Auntie Fox's behalf. Leaning on his crutch, the old man hobbled off to the tsar as fast as he could crawl.

"Honorable tsar," he said. "Auntie Fox has come with Bey Zlatum, and she wishes to ask if she might come before you."

"Let her come in," the tsar said.

After what seemed to be an eternity, the old man hobbled back and told the fox that she could go in to the tsar. Auntie Fox took her Bey Zlatum by the hand and began to speak to the tsar. "May God help us, tsar!"

"God be with you, Auntie," the tsar replied.

"Well, here I am," said the fox. "I've come as I promised."

"And where is your Bey Zlatum?" asked the tsar.

"Here he is, beside me," answered the fox.

"Why are you so dirty?" asked the tsar when he saw how muddy they were.

"Don't even ask us, your majesty!" the fox exclaimed. "We had an accident on the way. We came to a bridge, and to our misfortune the bridge broke. Bey Zlatum and I and the rest of our guests fell into the water below. Everyone drowned, except Bey Zlatum and myself. We were barely able to dig ourselves out of the mud. You can see how muddy we are. If you have a robe, please loan it to Bey Zlatum because he doesn't have a robe to change into, and it's a disgrace that he should go about looking so dirty."

"Don't worry, Auntie. Everything will be taken care of," the tsar answered. He ordered his servants to bring his nicest robe, and they changed Bey Zlatum's old, tattered robe for the new one.

Then Auntie Fox said, "As you see, honorable tsar, we encountered terrible trouble and all the wedding guests have perished. It would not be proper now for us to return home to gather guests again because Bey Zlatum's people are in mourning over their loved ones lost during the collapse of the bridge. For that reason, we ask that you provide us with 500 guests and whatever we need for the road."

"I will, my dear children," the tsar said, "because such an accident could happen to anyone, even to me. Don't worry about anything."

The tsar called his servants together and ordered them to invite all the lords of the land to be guests at the wedding.

Suppertime drew near, and the tsar and Bey Zlatum dined. Auntie Fox remained in the kitchen on the hearth picking over chicken bones.

After supper, Bey Zlatum went to his room to sleep and Auntie Fox went with him. Bey Zlatum lay in bed on a mattress and Auntie lay behind the stove.

The next day when the tsar and all his servants got up, Bey Zlatum rose from his bed and got dressed. He shouted to Auntie Fox to get up.

When dinnertime came, all the guests who were to be part of the wedding procession assembled. They dined with the tsar and Bey Zlatum. Halfway through the meal, the tsar called his daughter.

"Here is your spouse, my dear daughter," he said. "May you be happy forever, until the day you die. I give her to you, Bey Zlatum, my son-in-law. She is my only child. I wouldn't give her to anyone else but you. Take good care of her, and be happy with her."

"Well said!" a guest exclaimed in agreement.

When dinner was over, they began firing cannons, as is the custom during Bosnian weddings. The wedding guests sang merrily, but fear curled like a serpent around Bey Zlatum's heart. What would happen to him? He had no beautiful mansion to bring the guests to.

Whenever he was alone with Auntie Fox, he put on a worried look and said, "What will happen to me now, for goodness sake?"

"Don't be afraid," she kept reassuring him.

All of the guests sat in carriages by twos and threes. In one carriage sat the tsarevna and her maid of honor, and in another sat Bey Zlatum and Auntie Fox. While they were traveling, Bey Zlatum squirmed and fidgeted about the coach like a devil on a tree stump. Auntie Fox consoled him and tried to quiet him down, telling him he had nothing to fear.

When they had covered half the distance, Auntie Fox said to Bey Zlatum, "I'm taking a shortcut across the field. You go straight ahead, but don't go to your cottage. When you are near it, listen for my bark. Ride with your guests in the direction my bark is coming from."

As soon as Auntie had jumped out of the coach, she whisked into the forest.

In a short while, she came to a palace that belonged to two cruel giants. There were hardly any people left alive in the land because the giants had killed off almost everyone.

The giants came out to greet the fox. "What's roaring down the road like thunder?" they asked.

"My dear brother, the people of the world are coming to your palace to kill you," Auntie Fox replied. "I've come to warn you that you'll lose your heads if you wait here for them."

"Tell us quickly, you mangy fox, how we can escape," the giants bellowed rudely. "Advise us right now, or we'll make a fur collar out of you."

"Crawl under that pile of straw," said Auntie Fox.

They did as she said. After they had settled into the straw and quieted down, Auntie set the straw afire so that the two wicked giants perished. Auntie Fox was very happy, for she had rid the world of two terrible monsters, and she had freed the people of the land from their reign of terror.

Meanwhile, Bey Zlatum was thinking all sorts of things. "What a fool I am for staying alone like this. I think I'll run away, too." He kept talking to himself in this manner until he was near his own dilapidated cottage.

Here, he began listening. He heard Auntie barking in the forest far away, and he set out in the direction her voice was coming from.

When he got to her, he could not believe his eyes. A wonderful palace with marble pillars rose into the clouds. The wedding guests marveled at its beauty. Bey Zlatum, more than anyone else, wondered whose beautiful palace it was. If only I owned this magnificent dwelling, he said to himself, I wouldn't be ashamed to receive guests in it.

They stopped in the courtyard. Auntie Fox came out and said, "Well, at last you've arrived. Get out of the carriage."

Thinking that the owner of the palace would notice them, Bey Zlatum grew numb with fear and trembled like a leaf. But the palace was empty.

A little later, Auntie Fox told him the whole story in private. He was so delighted he could hardly contain himself.

Supper was prepared. The food was so abundant that no one went hungry. The guests enjoyed themselves, proposing toasts to each other and rejoicing in the good fortune of the tsar's daughter, for no one had dared to hope that Bey Zlatum would be so very rich.

The guests were entertained for three weeks, as was the custom. When the fourth week drew near, the guests went home, singing merrily and firing shots into the air.

When they reached the tsar's palace, they told the tsar that Bey Zlatum was a good husband, a good host, and a very rich man. The tsar was delighted to hear the good news.

Bey Zlatum was very happy in his palace with his darling bride. If he is still alive, you can be certain he is enjoying himself to this very day. ❀

The Snake Bridegroom

(Yugoslavia—Serbia)

Once upon a time there was a woman who had no children of her own. She was very poor and longed for a son or daughter to brighten her difficult life. The woman prayed to God to send her a child, even if the child should turn out to be a baby snake.

God heard her prayers, but instead of giving birth to a human child, the woman bore a little snake boy.

As soon as the snake was born, he slithered into the grass and disappeared. The unhappy woman grieved for the snake and wept constantly over her loss. Although God had granted her wish for a child, she did not know where her snake son had run off to or how he was faring.

After twenty years had passed, a snake suddenly appeared on the woman's doorstep and started talking to her. "I'm the little boy that God sent in answer to your prayers, the one who ran away from you into the grass. I've come back, Mother, so that you can ask on my behalf for the hand of the tsar's daughter in marriage."

The old woman was happy to see her offspring, but his request disturbed her. How could she, in her poverty, dare to ask for the tsar's daughter for her snake son?

The snake spoke to her again. "Go ahead, Mother. Don't worry about it, for you know that everyone has the right to ask for the girl of his choice. Even if the tsar doesn't give her to you, he won't take off your head. It doesn't hurt to ask. But remember, no matter what the tsar tells you, don't look back on your way home until you reach our house."

The snake's mother, her mind filled with doubt, set out to call upon the tsar. When she reached the tsar's palace, the servants did not want to permit her an audience with their sovereign. They distrusted her because of her ragged clothing and her poverty, but she begged so hard and so pitifully that they finally gave in and took her to see the tsar.

When the woman appeared before the ruler, she said, "Your majesty, there is your sword, and here is my head. I throw myself on your mercy, but first listen to my story. For a long time I had no little boy or girl of my own, so I prayed to God to send me a child, even if the child should turn out to be a snake. God heard my prayers, but instead of giving me a human child, he sent a little snake boy. As soon as my son was born, he ran off into the grass and disappeared. Twenty years have passed since that sad day, and my snake son has come home. He sent me to ask for your daughter's hand in marriage."

The tsar, thinking that the woman's poverty must have made her mad, laughed at her story. Then, to humor her, he said, "I will give my daughter to your son if he will make a bridge of pearls and precious stones extending from my palace to his home."

When the snake's mother heard the tsar's answer, she felt sorry for her son, who would certainly never be able to accomplish such an impossible task. Obeying her son's instructions, she returned home without looking back.

Then a miracle took place. As soon as the woman left the tsar's palace, a bridge of pearls and precious stones formed behind her. With every step she took, the jewel-studded bridge grew longer and longer. Not once did she forget her son's instructions. She never glanced back out of curiosity. And it was a very good thing that she did not, for if she had, the wonderful bridge that sparkled so brightly in the sun would have disappeared.

The mother told her snake son what the tsar had said.

"Mother," he instructed her, "go back to the tsar, and ask for his daughter's hand in marriage once again. But remember, no matter what the tsar gives you for an answer, don't look back on your way home."

The mother set out wearily. She came to the wonderful bridge. She was unable to believe her eyes. Perhaps now, she thought, the tsar will agree to give his daughter to my son. This thought made the long journey to the tsar's palace seem shorter.

Her heart filled with hope, she went before the tsar. She asked him whether he would give his daughter in marriage to her son now that the wonderful bridge had been built.

The tsar hemmed and hawed and searched for a way out of his predicament. "If your son builds a palace more beautiful than mine, I will give him my daughter," he finally pronounced sternly.

When the poor woman heard these words, her hopes were dashed. She returned home sadly. But she did not forget her son's instructions. Not once did she glance back.

When she reached home, there in place of her old, dilapidated cottage was a palace more beautiful than the tsar's. The woman's joy knew no bounds.

She told her snake son everything that the tsar had said.

"Go back, Mother, and see whether or not the tsar will give his daughter to me now. Don't forget, no matter what the tsar says, don't glance back until you get to our house."

The mother thought that surely this time the tsar would have to keep his word and give his daughter to her son in marriage.

When she went before the tsar, she said, "My son obeyed your command. He has a palace more beautiful than yours. Now will you give him your daughter?"

This time the tsar was ready with an answer. "If your son furnishes his palace more elegantly than mine, then I will give him my daughter."

The tired mother was becoming angry with the tsar. Perhaps the tsar intended to keep assigning impossible tasks forever so that her son would never win his bride. She stomped home angrily, but she remembered not to glance back.

When she reached home, she found to her surprise that her palace was furnished three times more elegantly than the tsar's. In the courtyard were golden birds, chickens, deer, and rabbits. The palace was filled with ornate, golden furniture. In fact, everything was gilded with gold so that it dazzled her eyes.

When the mother told the snake what the tsar had said, the snake told her, "Go to the tsar just one more time, Mother, and ask him if he will give me his daughter now."

Once again the snake's mother went to the tsar and informed him that her son's palace was furnished far more elegantly than his own.

Then the tsar turned to his daughter. "Daughter, now you may marry the snake, if you care to, because he lives in greater luxury than we do."

The tsar's daughter was very beautiful. She had rosy cheeks and dark hair. However, she also had a mind of her own. She was not ready to agree to marriage.

"Father," she said, "I can't marry someone I don't know."

Then the tsar sent for the snake to introduce him to his daughter, the tsarevna. The tsar's daughter was impressed with the snake's nice manners and kind words. She saw that he was far superior to the spoiled, haughty young men whom she knew, so she agreed to the marriage.

The snake made arrangements for the wedding. After the ceremony, he took the tsar's daughter away. The tsarevna's mother and sister, unable to understand how the girl could have fallen in love with a snake, wept for weeks.

To everyone's amazement, the young couple was very happy. Everyone predicted that the tsarevna would return home to her mother and father within a week, but she did not. She seemed to love the emerald-green snake very much.

Soon the rumor spread that the snake's wife had given birth to a baby boy. Her mother, sister, and the entire family were amazed. "How is it possible for a snake to be the father of a human being?" they asked.

"God granted our wish to have a little son," the snake's wife replied.

The tsarevna's answer failed to satisfy them, and her family remained as curious as ever about the miraculous birth.

Finally, her mother-in-law asked, "Daughter-in-law, how could my snake son be the father of a human being?"

"Oh, Mother," the girl replied, "he isn't a snake at all. He's a young man. There's no one on earth more handsome. Every evening he takes off his snakeskin, and in the morning he gets into it again. God isn't responsible for giving you a snake boy, as you thought. A wicked sorcerer cast a spell on him the moment he was born, and that's why he turned into a snake and ran away from you. He must live in the snake's skin until he dies. Please don't tell anyone the truth, or the sorcerer will take him away."

The snake's mother was very happy to hear that her son was really a human being, and she wanted to see him after he had come out of his snake's skin.

"Daughter-in-law, would it be possible to see what my son really looks like?" she asked.

"When we're alone together in our room, I'll take the key out of the lock. Then, when he begins removing his skin, you'll be able to look through the keyhole and see him," the daughter-in-law said.

The mother followed these instructions and saw that her son was a very handsome young man indeed. She began thinking about how to make him remain a young man forever.

One day she said to her son's wife, "Daughter-in-law, I've got an idea. Let's burn the snake's skin when my son takes it off. I'll heat the oven and throw the skin into the fire."

But the daughter-in-law answered, "Mother, I'm afraid that something will happen to him."

"Nothing will happen to him," his mother replied. "If his own human skin gets hot while we are burning his snake's skin, take some cold water and pour a little on him until his cast-off skin is burned up."

The girl agreed reluctantly. She was afraid that her mother-in-law's plan might not work.

The snake's mother heated the oven, and the young man came out of his snake's skin in the evening and lay down to sleep. While he was asleep, his mother and wife stole his cast-off skin and threw it into the oven.

As the skin began burning, the fire began to affect the snake man. His human skin felt as if it were burning, and he was in great pain. The two women kept pouring water over him to keep him alive.

The terrifying face of the evil sorcerer, who had enchanted the young man, appeared over his body like a ghost. Angry, hypnotic eyes glared at them. The mother and wife were afraid.

Suddenly the menacing head began to fade. As the pile of burning snake's skin grew smaller, the vision of the sorcerer's head became paler. Finally, it disappeared entirely. The spell had been broken.

When the heat abated and he awoke, the young man smelled the stench from the cast-off skin. He jumped to his feet. "What have you done? May God forgive you for your terrible deed! Where can I go like this?" he shouted.

His mother and wife started reassuring him. "You have had to wear the snake's skin for so long that you're beginning to think like a snake. It's better for you to look like a human being and to live among people."

Speaking in this manner, they finally managed to calm him down. After several days had passed, he had to admit that he liked being a human better than being a snake. He even wished that his mother and wife had thought up their clever plan sooner.

When the tsar heard that his son-in-law was really a handsome young man, he handed his kingdom over to him. The snake bridegroom became tsar, and he reigned happily ever after. ❖

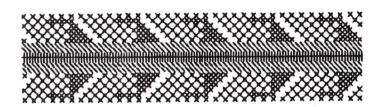

Part III

FAIRY TALES

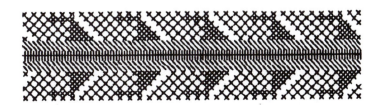

Škrat, the Wood Goblin

(Croatia)

There once lived a peasant who suffered misfortune every year. He could not make ends meet, so he accumulated one debt after another. He became heavily indebted to his rich neighbor, who showed no mercy in demanding that he return the money he borrowed right away. Because the peasant could not return the money, the rich man took him to court.

Early in the evening of the day when the peasant's property was to be sold to pay his debt, the despondent man was taking a walk in the forest. There, a hunter, whom he did not know, approached him and asked directions. The peasant told the hunter which direction to take and walked along with him to show him the way.

As they walked, they conversed about this and that. Finally, the peasant confided in the hunter concerning his troubles.

"I will help you if you give me something in return," the stranger said to him.

"I'll give you whatever you want," answered the peasant.

"Good," said the hunter. "I'll give you a sack full of gold. You'll be able to pay off your entire debt and still have some money left over. But you must give me that which you have at home and know nothing about."

What could it be that I have at home and know nothing about? wondered the peasant. What could it be? To the stranger, he said, "Just take whatever it is, sir. Whatever will be, will be, but you must help me."

"Fine," the hunter agreed. He gave the peasant a sack of gold coins and said, "In seven years, at this same time and on this same spot, you will hand over to me that which you have promised."

The peasant was a little perplexed as to why the stranger had decided everything so quickly. He could not figure out what it was he had at home, so he got worried. "Is there a way I can get out of giving you what you demand?" he asked.

The stranger laughed and said, "There is. If you find out what my name is before the appointed day, you can keep both the gold coins and that which you have promised me."

Then the stranger vanished without a trace, and the peasant remained standing on the spot with a sack in his hand. He did not think very much about the deal he had made or about the mysterious stranger but hurried home so that he could tell his wife about his great joy.

He entered the house and was shocked to see that in his absence a son had been born. When he had made the deal with the hunter, the peasant had not known that he had a son at home. Unwittingly, he had sold his son to the stranger.

After he understood what he had done, he worried, but did not lose hope. He had seven years to think up a way to save his son, seven years to inquire about the identity of the mysterious stranger.

The very next day he paid his debt to his neighbor. He still had plenty of money left over, as the stranger had promised. He managed the money well, and his possessions increased with each passing year. He built a new home. He had a great variety of crops, and his barns were loaded with an abundant harvest.

His son grew up healthy and strong. Moreover, all of his tenants liked him. Often, he would set his child on his lap and look at him for a long time. As he watched the boy, his heart grew heavier and heavier. He never told anyone how he had acquired his money.

The years passed—the first, the second, the third, the fourth, the fifth, and the sixth—until finally the seventh year came. As the day approached when he would have to give up his child to the menacing hunter, the peasant's mood worsened. His face became wrinkled because of his great worry. He avoided all friendships and roamed the forests alone.

Who was the stranger? He constantly racked his brain for answers. He inquired secretly throughout the entire country about the names of various hunters. He learned the names of many people, but the name he was searching for was not among them.

Finally, only three days remained—three days and then he had to give up his little son. The peasant left the house sadly and went into the forest. Darkness was falling when he came to the place where he had made a deal with the stranger seven years ago. Because of his great sorrow and concern, at first the miserable peasant did not notice where he was. Then it dawned on him that he was on the very spot where he had met the hunter. He was astonished by what he saw.

At the place where they had stood seven years ago, a stake was burning and a little man was hopping around it. He was dressed in a crimson coat and green pants. He wore green boots and a green cap. The peasant's mouth fell open. Without blinking an eye, he stared at the little monster.

The little man began singing with great joy.

> Ho, ho, ho,
> The peasant doesn't know
> That Škrat's my name;
> Wood goblining's my game.
> I'll take his son,
> And off I'll run.
> Ho, ho, ho!

The peasant heard everything the little man said, and he laughed to himself happily. Hey, little fellow, he thought to himself, if that is so, then now I know who you are. He turned around and went home.

For two days the peasant was in a very good mood. As he waited for the hunter to come, he went about his business as usual.

On the evening of the third day, the expected guest arrived. The family had just eaten supper and was still assembled. The hunter entered the door and approached the master of the house.

"Let's find out if you know who I am, boss."

"Oh, how could I fail to know the name of a wood goblin like you, Škrat," the peasant shouted.

Quick as lightning, Škrat turned around and flew through the door in a rage. As he was leaving, he grabbed a corner of the house, and it broke off.

The peasant's son remained behind. The peasant's big, beautiful house remained, too, but not one bricklayer succeeded in restoring the corner that Škrat had broken off. To this day the house still stands with one corner missing. ✿

The Nightingale Empress

(Yugoslav Albanian)

There once was a king who had three sons. More than anything else in the world, the king liked to go to the mosque to pray. Therefore, he decided to build the most beautiful mosque on earth.

When the builder completed the work, the king went to the new mosque to pray to Allah. While he was praying, a dervish, who is a Muslim dedicated to a life of poverty and purity, came up to him. "The mosque is beautiful," he said. "What a shame it is that the prayers said within it are said in vain, for Allah doesn't hear them."

When the king learned that Allah would not hear the prayers said in the mosque, he was angry. He had the mosque destroyed and commanded that another one, more beautiful and splendid than the first, be built.

After the mosque was built as he had commanded, the king went into the new mosque to pray. Once again the dervish approached him and said, "The mosque is beautiful. What a shame it is that the prayers said within it are said in vain."

The king grew angry and destroyed the mosque. He had yet another mosque, more lovely than the second one, built. However, the dervish continued to say the same thing.

Angry and upset, the king returned to his palace to consider whether or not to destroy the third mosque, in which prayer still was not heard by

Allah. If he built a fourth mosque, his entire fortune would be spent and nothing would be left to build a fifth mosque.

His sons approached him while he was in this upset state of mind and asked him what was bothering him.

"I'm angry," the king said to his sons. "And why wouldn't I be angry? I had three mosques built and spent nearly my entire fortune on them, yet Allah can't hear the prayers said in even one of them." He told his sons that every time he had gone to the mosque to pray an old dervish had told him that his prayers were said in vain.

His sons gave him the following instructions. "Go to the mosque tomorrow and pray. We will conceal ourselves and when we catch sight of the dervish, we'll seize him. Then we'll find out what he's up to."

They did just that. The king went to the mosque to pray, and his sons lay in ambush outside the mosque.

Suddenly the dervish appeared and spoke to the king again. "The mosque is beautiful, but what a shame it is that the prayers said within it are said in vain."

As soon as the dervish went out the door, the princes seized him. "Why do you keep saying that the mosque is beautiful but that prayers said within it are said in vain?"

"The mosque *is* beautiful," said the dervish, "more beautiful than any other in the land. However, if the Nightingale Empress were found and placed in the mosque, it would be so perfect that it would be the most beautiful mosque in the world. Then the prayers said in the mosque would be heard by Allah."

The princes asked the dervish where the magic bird lived. "I have heard of the nightingale," he told them, "but I don't know where she can be found."

The sons released the dervish and went to their father to tell him what the holy man had said. They promised to go out into the world to find the magic bird and not to return without her. They got ready and set out hurriedly on their journey to search for the Nightingale Empress.

After traveling for ten days, they arrived at a crossroads where four roads met. A square stone with an inscription on it stood at the crossroads. On two sides was written: "Whoever sets out in this direction will return." On the other two sides was written: "Whoever goes in this direction will not return alive."

The three brothers sat for a while and deliberated. They decided to go their separate ways and that each one should select his own direction. The youngest brother chose the direction from which no one had returned. The other two brothers chose the direction from which people had returned.

Before parting, they removed all their rings, placed them on the stone, and came to the agreement that whoever returned first and found his brothers' rings would go after the others and find them. Then the brothers kissed, and each went his own way.

The two older brothers came to a city and decided to stay there. One became an innkeeper, and the other became a barber. They lived peacefully and gave no more thought to the reason they had set out on their journey.

The youngest brother, who had gone down the dangerous road, came to a wasteland where there were neither houses, nor people, but only wild beasts and poverty.

While walking down the road, he came upon a wild woman. Her hair was tangled and twisted. She aggressively took the prince by the hand and ran it through her hair, as if it were a comb. The harder she tried to comb her hair with his hand, the more tangled her hair became. The young man took pity on her for exerting such effort in vain. He took out his comb and began combing her hair slowly and neatly.

After he had combed and cleaned her hair, the wild woman asked him, "How can I thank you for the service you have done me?"

"I'm not looking for any thanks," the young man told her, "but I have a question I would like to ask."

"Well, what would you like to know?" asked the wild woman.

"I am eager to know where the Nightingale Empress can be found. Has she ever passed through the forest here?"

"We don't have a bird like that here," said the woman. "You had better return home. This is a veritable wilderness. Even I, a wild woman, don't dare cross to the other side of the mountain, because the beasts there are even wilder."

"Well, I must go there," the young man said, "and may Allah grant me the good fortune of a hero!"

He said good-bye to the wild woman and set out over the mountain. Soon he came to a house and entered it. It turned out to be a lynx's house. The lady lynx was mixing dough to make bread.

The young man greeted her. As soon as she caught sight of him, she shouted, "Run away from here, unfortunate boy, if your head is dear to you. Soon my husband, the lynx, will come home, and he will eat you up."

"Since I am already here, you can do whatever you like with me," the young man said, and he remained where he was.

When the time came to put the bread into the oven, the lady lynx did not have anything other than her bare paws to dig out the embers of the fire. She usually burned her paws so badly after making bread that she had to lay abed for eight days, suffering until her wounds healed.

When the young man saw how badly her paws were burned, he jumped up and said, "Let me start the fire for you."

He tore off a leafy tree branch and tied it to the broom. Then, he swept out the hearth with the broom and started the fire. He placed the loaves of bread into the oven and covered the bread pan.

The lady lynx watched how he placed the bread in the oven without burning his hands as if it were a miracle. She was very happy to learn this skill and felt sorry that her husband would devour the young man when he returned home.

She began considering how she might save the prince. She removed the bread from the oven, gave the young man something to eat, and hid him in the oven after it had cooled down.

Early that evening the lynx returned home. He was amazed that his wife was not lying abed crying over her burned paws, as she usually did after baking bread, but instead was walking around in good health.

Infuriated, the lynx shouted at his wife, "Why didn't you bake bread today?"

"I did," she answered, "but I didn't burn myself."

"Why didn't you burn yourself?"

"I learned how to bake bread the right way. What would you say if I told you there was a man who taught me how to bake bread without burning myself?"

"I would thank him and hold him dear, just as if he were my own brother."

The lady lynx summoned the young man from the oven and led him to her husband, who thanked him very much for his kindness and gave him a brotherly kiss. "Why have you come here?" the lynx asked.

"I'm on a journey in search of the Nightingale Empress, but no one can tell me where to find the magic bird. Have you heard where the bird lives?"

The lynx replied, "The bird isn't here, but I have a brother who is very old. Because of his age, his eyelashes have grown so long he can't see anything through them. Perhaps he has heard of the magic bird at some time during his long life. Go to him, and ask him."

The lynx explained how the prince could find the house and how he should behave when he arrived there. "The lion is my brother," he said. "His old, blind wife, the lioness, sits in front of the house all day and guards it. Approach her slowly and lie down in her lap like a child. Caress and embrace her. She will ask, 'Who is caressing and embracing me?' You reply, 'Mother, I am your son, and I am embracing you like a child.' Then the old lion in the house will ask, 'Who has come to see us?' You reply, 'I am the friend of your brother, the lynx, and he sent me to ask a question.' 'Approach,' he will say. You go up to him and comb his eyelashes so that he can see, and then ask him where the Nightingale Empress can be found. If he doesn't know, then return to me."

The lynx said a friendly good-bye, and the young man did what he had been told. He asked the lion if he knew the whereabouts of the Nightingale Empress.

"There is no such bird here," the lion said. "You must follow the road to your right to find the magic bird. But you'd better return home, because there are so many wild beasts and evil spirits where the magic bird lives that no one dares go there except me, king of the animals."

The young man took leave of the lion and wished him every happiness. He set out down the very road the lion had warned him to avoid. He had gone a great distance and was very tired when three eagles flew toward him and opened their beaks to devour him.

The young man pulled out a sword and wounded one in the wing, the second in the leg, and the third in the beak. The eagles, understanding that they could not overcome him, flew off and went their own way. The young man went on.

He continued on and on until he caught sight of a house in the middle of a great field. He rushed toward it. There he found an old woman who had just baked a round, flat bread on the hearth.

When the old woman spied the young man, she screamed for help and shouted, "Why have you come here, son? Oh, your unfortunate mother! When my girls return, they'll eat you alive!"

"I have already crossed the threshold of your house," answered the young man, "so I will remain. Do whatever you think best, Granny."

The old woman took pity on the young man. She removed the bread from the hearth. She fed him and then began setting three tables in the middle of the house. She put a pitcher of water and a loaf of bread in the center of each table. Then she hid the young man in a cupboard. She left the door ajar so that he could see and hear what was happening outside.

After some time had passed, the young man saw an eagle with a wounded wing fly through the window. It went up to one of the pitchers of water and began washing up. As it washed, its feathers fell away and it was transformed into a girl.

In the blink of an eye another eagle with a wounded leg flew up, washed itself, and was transformed into a girl. Then, the third eagle arrived with a wounded beak, and it, too, turned into a girl.

After they had turned into young women, they said to their mother, "Mom, we smell a human being!"

"You just came from the humans' world, and their scent is still in your nose."

While the girls were eating dinner, their mother asked, "What would you do, children, to a person to whom I had given shelter?"

"Unfortunately, I have been wounded in the wing, so I wouldn't be able to do him any harm," said the oldest.

"Unfortunately, I have been wounded in the leg, so I wouldn't be able to do him any harm," said the middle girl.

"Unfortunately, I have been wounded in the beak, so I wouldn't be able to do him any harm" said the youngest.

Then the old woman pulled the young man out of the cupboard. "I am the one who wounded you. Please forgive me," he said.

The girls were happy that they had found the young man who had displayed such daring and bravery in fighting them on the battlefield. They asked him why he had come to their land.

"I am on a journey to find the Nightingale Empress," said the young man. "So far, everyone I have asked has neither seen nor heard of the magic bird."

"We know about the Nightingale Empress," they told him, "but you must go there on foot. It will take you three years to reach her, and you may lose your life on the way."

"How can I get there?" the young man asked.

"If you obey us, we will go there with you, and within an hour we will capture the Nightingale Empress."

"How can I repay you for the favor?" the young man asked.

"Stay with us for three months. You will be a servant to each of us for one month."

Thus, they came to an agreement. The young man served them for three months. After the time had passed, the girls left and flew to where the Nightingale Empress lived.

The bird was located in a golden cage in the palace of the *vila* queen. There were 500 guards around the palace and in the courtyard. A wolf guarded the first door, a lynx guarded the second door, and a lion guarded the third door, through which one entered the palace.

At night when everyone in the palace was asleep and the palace guards were dozing, the eagles dropped the young man slowly into the courtyard. He crept into the palace hall. In the hall, he saw four lit and four unlit lamps. The former had burned down so low that they were ready to go out, so the prince immediately ignited the other four and extinguished the ones that were burning out.

Then he grabbed the cage with the magic bird and went out the door slowly. As soon as he appeared at the door, the guards awoke and attacked him.

His friends, the eagles, grabbed him quickly, raised him into the air, and carried him home. He stayed at their house for some time.

When he finally decided to set out for home, he asked the girls to see him off. Once again, they carried him. They let him down at the crossroads, where he and his brothers had parted.

Finding his and his brother rings there, he knew they had not returned. He set out to look for them.

He found one working as a barber. The other was working as an innkeeper. "Come, brothers, let's return home," he said, "for I have found the Nightingale Empress."

And so all three of them set out. On the way, they became thirsty, but there was no spring in the vicinity. They came across a well, but they had nothing with which to draw the water from the well. They asked the youngest brother to go down into the well and draw up some water.

They lowered him into the well with a rope, but they did not pull him back up. Instead, they cut the rope with a knife, and the youngest brother fell into the well. Luckily, the water was not deep. It came just up to the young man's chest, so he did not drown.

The two older brothers, thinking that their younger brother had drowned, took the magic bird. When they arrived home, they gave it to their father, boasting about how much they had suffered on its account.

When the father asked about their younger brother, they said that he had squandered his money in drink and that he had become an unemployed bum who wandered from city to city.

From the moment the brothers had thrown their younger brother into the well, the Nightingale Empress had been silent and had not sung one song, even though her voice was sweeter than that of any other bird.

After the brothers had bragged to their father about finding the magic bird, the *vila* queen came searching for the Nightingale Empress to bring her back to the home from which she had been taken. Having heard the oldest brother bragging, she asked him where he had found the bird.

"I fcund her on a cypress tree," he said.

The *vila* became infuriated when she heard his lie. She insulted him in front of his subjects, who beat him with a stick when they learned that he was not the one who had captured the bird.

When the middle brother saw what had happened to his older brother, he fell to his knees and knelt before his father. He told him the truth about how the youngest brother had found the bird and how they had thrown him into the well to drown and had taken away the nightingale.

When the *vila* queen heard the real story, she went to the well and found the young man, barely alive. He was breathing slowly, but not speaking. In this lifeless state she brought him to his father's palace. When the young prince regained consciousness and began speaking, the Nightingale Empress began singing so sweetly that everyone melted with delight.

Hearing the nightingale sing, the old king rejoiced. He took the bird into the mosque, which now had no more shortcomings. After saying his prayers, he sang the praises of his youngest son and the *vila* who had saved him.

The king asked the *vila* for her hand in marriage to his son, and she agreed to marry the young prince. They lived happily for many years. When the old king died, the young prince and his *vila* bride ruled the kingdom. ✿

The Water Sprite

(Slovenia)

There once was a boy who longed to go swimming. Although he begged and begged, his parents told him it was too dangerous. One day when the floodwaters rose, he just could not bear to stay home. Instead, he went to the river, to which his mother and father had forbidden him to go.

Once at the river, he got undressed and plunged into the water. The current was very strong and carried him away. The boy struggled, beating the water with his arms and waving his hands in every direction.

He shouted and wailed at the top of his voice until the Water Sprite, who lived at the bottom of the river, heard him. And it is a good thing that he heard him because at that moment water was filling the boy's nose and mouth, and he was losing consciousness.

After the Water Sprite rushed up to him, he searched for a place where the boy could sleep. He churned up the water and carried the boy down deep into the river. Indeed, the Water Sprite had never before brought a living being to his watery kingdom. As a rule, anyone who fell into the water drowned immediately. But the Water Sprite was unusually drawn to the small boy. He felt sorry to see him drown, so he decided to save him. After all, he was lonely in his spacious kingdom. The idea of making friends with this nice little boy made him happy.

He took the boy in his arms and carried him to a splendid city at the bottom of the river. No living person had ever crossed the threshold of his palace. He placed the boy in a bed that was made of crystal and stood in the middle of a crystal room. Then he left quietly and hid, waiting for the child to awaken.

When the boy awoke, he looked around and saw that he was lying on a crystal bed in the middle of a crystal room. Next to the bed was a night-stand. On the nightstand were many toys, all made of crystal. The boy was captivated by their beauty and radiance. He reached for the crystal toys and began playing with them. But suddenly he remembered home, and he burst into tears.

The Water Sprite came running up to him and asked, "Why are you crying, little boy?"

"I am crying for my home," the boy answered, and he continued crying inconsolably.

"Is your home more beautiful than the wealth you see before you?" asked the Water Sprite.

"It is more beautiful," the boy replied, crying all the louder.

The Water Sprite saw that what he said did not help, so he left the child alone. Exhausted from crying so hard, the boy fell asleep.

Then the Water Sprite came and carried the boy in his arms to another room. When the child awoke, he looked around and noticed that he was lying on a bed made of silver, which was located in the middle of a room with silver walls, ceiling, and floor.

A nightstand stood next to the bed, and on it were toys made of pure silver. Fascinated, the boy looked at the wealth. Then he reached for the toys and began playing, but the play soon bored him. He remembered his brothers and sisters, with whom he had played at home, and he cried bitterly.

The Water Sprite came running. "Why are you crying now, my little child?"

"I'm crying for my brothers and sisters," the boy replied, and he cried still louder.

Because he could not comfort the boy, the Water Sprite left. Then the boy slept soundly. Once again the Water Sprite took him up in his arms and carried him to a third room.

When the little boy awoke, he saw that the Water Sprite had moved him to a bed made of pure gold, which stood in the middle of a room built of pure gold. Everything in the room was made of gold—the nightstand, chair, and toys. The boy had already heard a great deal about magic treasures of gold, but never could he have imagined such radiance as that which was blinding him now.

Delighted, he reached for the golden toys and began playing with them. His play did not last long. His mother and father came to mind, and he began crying loudly once again.

Having heard his cry, the Water Sprite rushed up to him and asked, "Why are you crying, little boy?"

"I miss my mother and father," the boy answered, and he cried louder and louder.

"Are your mother and father really dearer to you than pure gold?" asked the Water Sprite, who had never known a mother or father, sisters or brothers.

"Yes," the child said.

The Water Sprite collected all the pearls that were hidden at the bottom of his watery kingdom. He kept spilling them before the boy until the pile reached the ceiling. Then, he asked, "Are your mother and father dearer than these pearls?"

The boy had to shut his eyes so that he would not be blinded by so much radiance. The treasures shone and glowed as if the room were on fire. But the boy replied, "You labor in vain trying to find a price for my mother and father. They are dearer than gold and pearls, dearer than the whole world."

The Water Sprite saw that the child could not be consoled with anything. He waited until the boy fell asleep and carried him carefully in his arms out of the water. He put him down, asleep, on the bank of the river. Here, his poor clothing, which he had taken off before plunging into the water, was awaiting him. The Water Sprite searched for the boy's pockets, filled them with pure gold and pearls, and left.

The boy awoke and saw that he was lying on the riverbank near the water. He stood up and got dressed. Indeed, he did not know whether he had only dreamed everything that had happened with the Water Sprite or if he had really experienced it. But when he put his hand in his pocket and felt the gold and pearls, he knew he had not been dreaming.

He rushed home to his mother and father and sisters and brothers. He found all of them weeping because they thought that he had drowned. When they saw him, their happiness knew no bounds. Now there was no lack of gold or pearls, and misfortune had been avoided.

They began living happily. They built a new house and were very proud of it. From then on, the boy went swimming only when there was no flood, and then just in the shallow water, where the Water Sprite never goes.

The Water Sprite returned to his watery kingdom and was terribly sad. Now he understood that people possessed a great fortune that he did not—mothers, fathers, sisters, and brothers.

He was so sad that he cried nonstop for three days. His tears caused the waters to swell and run over onto the riverbanks, as they do during a flood. Then, feeling a great emptiness in his life, he began searching every nook and cranny of his kingdom, hoping to find a treasure that was comparable to the love the boy had for his family. He came to understand that the treasure of family love, which he had discovered when he met the boy, had no equal. ❀

The Young Man and His Vampire Brother

(Yugoslav Romany)

There once was a man who had a wife and son, but his wife died and he married another woman. The stepmother, as is often the case, could not stand her stepson. They quarreled frequently. Finally, she gave her husband an ultimatum. "Either I leave, or your son leaves."

Because he loved his wife, the man gave his son twelve dinars and told him to go away. The boy traveled to a town where he came upon a dead man, whom no one wanted to bury, lying in the market place. Passers-by were spitting on the corpse. When the young man asked why they were doing so, he was told that the dead man had owed a great deal of money and had died without paying his debt.

Feeling sorry for the deceased, the young man took the money his father had given him and paid off everything the dead man owed. With the money that was left over, he had him laid to rest in style.

Afterward, he set out for another town. The road he traveled passed by the cemetery where the corpse had been buried. As he neared the cemetery, the man he had buried, now a vampire, approached him in disguise. "Where are you going, brother?" he asked.

"I'm going to look for a job," the young man answered.

The disguised vampire offered to go with him. They walked on until they came to another town. In this town, the daughter of the pasha, a Turkish official, had died. They had placed her in a chapel, where a different person guarded her each night. Mysteriously, whoever stood guard was found dead by dawn.

"Agree to stand guard over the pasha's daughter for three days and nights," the vampire said to his adopted brother. "Here is the Holy Scripture. While you are standing guard, put it above your head and keep looking at it. Don't take your eyes off it, or you too will be dead by dawn."

The young man did as the vampire advised, and nothing happened to him the first night. The second night passed in the same manner. On the third evening, his adopted brother said, "Remember, don't take your eyes off the Holy Scripture. As soon as the cock begins crowing, the pasha's daughter will rise from her coffin. As soon as she rises, lie down in the coffin in her place."

The young man did as his vampire brother had advised. As soon as the cock began crowing, the girl came out of the coffin. He got in quickly and lay down in her place.

The girl began imploring him to move so that she could lie down again, but he did not move. Instead, he continued to stare only at the Holy Scripture.

When dawn came, the spell that had been placed on the pasha's daughter was broken because she could not return to her coffin. The young man led the girl to her father. When the pasha saw her, he was very happy. "What do you want me to do for you?" he asked the young man.

"I will be satisfied with whatever you give me," said the young man.

The pasha gave the young man his daughter's hand in marriage and found employment for him and his vampire brother in his office.

After some time had passed, the young man wanted to visit home. He bid his father-in-law farewell and set out by cart with an armed escort for home.

On the way, he came to a tavern. At first he saw no one within. Then he noticed that two people were sitting, drinking coffee.

As soon as the young man entered the tavern, a cup of coffee appeared before him. He did not see anyone bring it. It appeared by itself.

After he had finished the coffee, the two men talked him into playing cards. The two men cheated shamelessly, but the young man did not notice. In this manner, they took all his money, his cart, and his escort. He was left penniless.

Without anything to his name and with nowhere to go, he went back to his native land and was hired as a swineherd. His wife, the pasha's daughter, waited for a long time for her husband to return. Giving up hope of his ever returning, she set out with his vampire brother to search for him.

They came to the tavern, where the young man had played cards. The two men who had persuaded him to gamble were there.

The vampire brother asked them to play cards. As it turned out, they too were vampires. The vampire brother noticed their deceitful tricks right away. He began cheating too and took everything they had from them, as well as that which they had taken from the young man.

He and the pasha's daughter continued on their way in search of the young man. After a long time had passed, they found him guarding swine on the side of a mountain.

When the young man saw them, he began running away out of shame, but his vampire brother caught up with him and grabbed him. Then they bathed and dressed him so that he looked like he had before.

When they returned home, the vampire asked that what they had earned be divided equally between them. The young man agreed, and the vampire divided the money and possessions into two equal parts.

Then a question arose regarding how to divide the young man's wife into two parts. The vampire brother swung his knife and cut her down the middle into two equal parts.

The Young Man and His Vampire Brother

A serpent crawled out of the place where he had cut her. The vampire brother wasted no time in killing the serpent.

Then he said, "I am the dead man whose debt you paid. Therefore, I have rewarded you for your good deed. I have given you everything you deserve. I arranged for you to marry the pasha's daughter. I saved you from the two cheating vampires who stole your fortune, and I rid your wife of the evil serpent that dwelled within her. I have permission to stay on earth only for forty days. Today is the fortieth day, so I must return home."*

And so it came to pass that they parted. The vampire brother returned to the kingdom of the dead because his time on earth was up. ❁

* Orthodox Christians believe the dead roam the earth for forty days before leaving for heaven.

The Twelve Crumbs

(Yugoslavia—Serbia)

Once upon a time there was a tsar who lived happily in his palace with his wife and young son. Then his wife died suddenly, and he was left alone with his son, who cried all the time for his mother.

One day when the tsar was getting ready to go hunting, his little son threw his arms around his neck and began crying even harder than usual. The tsar felt sorry for the little tsarevich and decided to make him happy by marrying again. He resolved to find a kind woman, who would live with them and watch over the child. Somehow he managed to dry his son's tears, and he went off hunting.

While walking in the forest, the tsar happened upon a well where a pretty, rosy-cheeked woman was scooping water into twelve gourds. The tsar wondered why she was filling the gourds, and he asked her about it.

The woman smiled. "This is how I earn my supper," she said. "For every gourd of water I scoop, I get a crumb of bread. I earn twelve crumbs a day."

"Are twelve crumbs a day enough for you to live on?" asked the tsar.

"It's too much for me alone," she answered, "but I feed my little daughter first, then myself. It's just enough for both of us."

The tsar was astonished. He had never met such a humble, unselfish woman before. She would be good for my little boy, he thought.

He told her that he was the tsar, and he asked her to marry him. Of course she agreed right away.

The tsar brought her to his palace and married her that very day. She became his tsaritsa.

The new tsaritsa's daughter was younger than the tsar's son. The children got along well together and were well taken care of. The little tsarevich watched over his new little sister carefully, for she was very young and fragile looking. He kissed her when she bruised her knee and protected her from danger. The little tsarevich grew to love his sister with all his heart.

Whenever the tsar brought something nice home to the palace, such as a basket of ripe plums or red apples, he gave the gift to the children, and they divided it equally and amicably.

But the tsaritsa began to dislike life at the palace. She led a life of ease, quite different from her previous existence of honest, hard work. Because she had nothing to do, she began to brood and to think dark thoughts.

Why should my daughter share with the tsar's son when it is possible for her to have everything for herself? she wondered. So the bored woman plotted against the boy. She decided to make the tsar hate his son so that he would drive him away from home.

Becoming more and more inclined toward evil, the woman put her plan into action. She told her husband that she had dreamed the same terrible dream every day for several days and that she was troubled by it.

"In my dream your son grows up and turns against you," she told the tsar. "He seizes the throne and sends you and me and my daughter to the fields to work as day laborers."

The tsar was disturbed by his wife's story. When the evil woman saw his alarmed look, she continued filling his head with her account of the prophetic dream. Every time she told the story, it became more dreadful. Finally, the frightened tsar decided to banish his son from the palace to prevent the dream from coming true.

And so the tsarevich, who had already grown to be a handsome young man, had to disguise himself as an ordinary commoner and travel around the world. He was very sad indeed that his father had treated him so badly.

One day, during his travels, he spent the night near a cave where there lived an old hermit who wore a long, white beard down to his waist.

At midnight the tsarevich heard screams coming from the cave. He was frightened, but he recovered quickly and thought, Whoever is screaming is probably doing so because of some great misfortune.

He ran to the cave quickly and saw the hermit lying there. The old man seemed to be sick and thirsty, and he was screaming at the top of his lungs.

The tsar's son ran to the creek, scooped water into his cupped hands, and ran up the hill toward the cave. On the way, he fell on his knees and hurt himself, but he managed to bring a little water to the old man.

The hermit was very pleased by the young man's kindness. "Son, I'm not screaming because I'm sick and thirsty," he said, "but because there is so much evil and misfortune in the world. Now I'm happy because I've found someone who cares about a man sorrowing in solitude. Because you have helped me so kindly, ask for anything, and I'll give it to you if it is in my power to do so."

The tsarevich told the old hermit all about his wicked stepmother and how she had tricked his father. "Grief is killing me," he said. "If you know a remedy for it, I beg you to tell me."

The hermit handed him a little shepherd's flute and said, "No sooner said than done. This little flute will cheer you up. When you play it, your heart will dance. Every living creature around you will dance as long as the flute is singing."

The tsarevich thanked him warmly and went on. He could hardly wait to be alone so that he could play the flute.

He walked on and on. When he saw that no one else was near, he took the flute out of his knapsack to try it out. His heart began to dance with joy. He saw a squirrel high up in a tree hopping among the branches to the tune of his flute.

The tsarevich traveled around the world, far and wide. Finally, he found a job tending sheep for a wealthy man. His master treated him well, but when he remembered his father and home, he grew sad.

When his grief became too much to bear, he played a tune on his flute. He was always very careful, however, not to play the flute in the pasture near the sheep, for if the sheep heard the playing, they would leave the pasture and dance off into the forest.

One evening when he was returning home with the sheep, the tsarevich heard a loud wailing in the distance. When he arrived at his master's house, he found that a great misfortune had occurred.

His master had come across a group of *vilas* dancing a round dance called the *kolo* on the side of a mountain. These fairies never allow humans to watch their dancing. When they discovered that a mortal had seen them, the queen of the *vilas* gouged out both of the master's eyes. Now he and his family were lamenting his fate.

The tsarevich was horrified. He decided to set out in search of his master's eyes. That night he left his sheep, taking with him a sack filled with bread, salt, and onions. He put his flute into the sack too and went to the place his master had described when he told about his unfortunate meeting with the wicked *vilas*. The tsarevich told no one what he was doing or where he was going.

When he came to the spot, he found the queen of the *vilas* lying in the middle of a clearing on the mountainside. Twelve beautiful *vilas* were braiding and unbraiding her hair, and her braids shone in the moonlight like gold.

As he approached, they stopped braiding the queen's hair. The queen, who had appeared to be asleep until then, opened her eyes. The wicked women sensed his presence.

The tsarevich remembered an old riddle about *vilas*: "Who is born on a mountain, nourished with dew, and tanned by the sun?" They were beautiful women but dangerous and evil too.

He put his hand into his sack quickly and took out the flute. He began playing, slowly at first, then faster and faster. As he recovered from his fear, his playing became bolder and louder.

The *vilas* looked at each other in surprise and started giggling. They formed a ring to dance the *kolo*, and their feet began flying as if they were possessed. The tsarevich would not stop playing, and the dancing *vilas* could not catch their breath.

On and on they danced until their queen shouted, "I can't go on!" She tried to leave the *kolo*, but she could neither break away nor stop dancing. The evil spirits realized that they were in trouble.

"Whoever you are, we beg you to stop," they shouted.

"Show me where you have hidden my master's eyes," the tsarevich demanded.

The queen of the *vilas* swore to God that she did not have his master's eyes, but the young man did not for a moment believe her. He played on.

Finally, she said, "Go to the fir tree over which the moon is shining the brightest and take a golden bag made of leather from a hollow in the tree. In the leather bag, you'll find a silver box. In the silver box, you'll find some cotton, and in the cotton are the eyes you're looking for."

He did as the queen said, but he did not let the *vilas* out of his sight the entire time. As soon as they got a notion to move, he blew into the flute, and they began jumping about frantically. He went up to the fir tree, took the golden bag made of leather out of the hollow, and found the silver box inside. In the box he found the cotton, and nestled in the cotton were his master's eyes.

The tsarevich gave a shout of joy and returned to his master's house, playing his flute and singing all the way.

After the tsarevich returned his master's eyes to him, the blind man regained his sight. He embraced his servant, ran over to his treasure chest, and sprinkled gold on the young man.

"Take this as a reward for what you've done for me," the happy man said.

The tsarevich refused the reward. Suddenly, he remembered his father and his little stepsister, and he decided that it was time to travel on. He said that he wanted nothing except a good horse and a hero's weapons, for he was content to travel around the world doing good deeds.

His master gladly gave him everything he asked for, and the tsarevich began to wander around the world once again. He rescued many tsarevnas from terrible dragons. He fed the poor and freed those imprisoned unjustly. It was rumored far and wide that a brave young man was fighting battles for those in trouble and defending the weak against the powerful. First one, then another, called on him for help. Both simple men and wealthy tsars came to the tsarevich.

One day a summons came from his father, the tsar. He sent word to the young warrior without realizing that he was his son. "We have heard about you and your heroism," he wrote. "In the name of God, we ask for your help. A fire-breathing dragon has come to our kingdom, and he asks that we give him our daughter and our kingdom. We sent our bravest champions to fight him, but he killed them as if their strength were a mere joke. Please help us, and in return you may have anything in my kingdom that you desire."

When he heard that his father needed help, the tsarevich set out for home. On the way, he kept wondering who his father's daughter might be. He suspected that she was none other than the girl his stepmother had brought to the palace when she married his father. Perhaps it was the little stepsister who was so dear to him. If so, he was especially eager to help her.

Finally, he arrived in front of the tsar's palace. He found everything as he had left it, except that his father had aged greatly, as had the servants and his evil stepmother. But her daughter had grown into a beautiful young lady, whose happiness was now threatened by the wicked dragon.

He greeted his father politely. No one recognized the tsarevich, and he did not reveal his identity.

Early the next morning, he set out to meet the fire-breathing dragon. As soon as the dragon saw him, the beast rushed upon him screaming, "You are the one I have long been searching for."

The dragon shot arrows at him, but the tsarevich's horse kneeled down, and the arrows flew over his head.

Then the tsarevich threw a spear, but it broke in two and did no damage to the enraged beast. Eventually, the tsarevich broke all his weapons in his fight with the dragon, and he was left empty-handed. The dragon laughed maliciously and went directly toward him.

Suddenly, the tsarevich remembered his magic flute. He grabbed it and began playing. Every living creature within earshot started dancing.

The dragon squealed and began to tremble. As the flute sang, he began to shrink. He grew smaller and smaller, and the fire roaring from his nostrils became a mere wisp of smoke.

One moment he was the size of the tsarevich's horse. The next moment he was the size of a dog. Then he became as small as a warty toad, hopping about in a temper tantrum.

The tsarevich played on, and the dragon grew so small that there was nothing left of him but a little dancing bubble that belligerently jumped up and down.

The tsarevich quickly ran up and pressed the little bubble with his left foot. When the bubble burst, the dragon's evil power disappeared. Everyone was happy to learn that the wicked dragon was dead.

The tsar embraced the young man and asked him who he was and where he had come from. Only then did the tsarevich reveal his secret. He told his father everything that had happened to him.

The tsar became angry with his wife for plotting against his son, and he wanted to have her executed immediately. But the tsarevich pleaded for her life to be spared. Even though the woman had been cruel to him, and even though her lies had caused him great grief, he would not let his kind stepsister see her mother harmed. To repay cruelty with cruelty would be foolish indeed.

The tsar gave in to his son's wishes, but insisted that the tsaritsa be punished. He divorced her and ordered her to return to the mountain from which she had come. Once again she would have to fill twelve gourds with well water every day to earn her twelve crumbs.

Because the evil woman's beautiful daughter was no longer the tsarevich's sister, the tsar gave the girl to his son in marriage. God's will was done, just as it always is done in fairy tales. Justice and goodness prevailed. ❁

The Devil and His Apprentice

(Yugoslavia—Serbia)

There once lived a man who had only one son. One day the son said, "Father, what shall we do? I can't live in such terrible poverty. I must go out into the world to learn a trade. Nowadays the man who knows a trade has a better life than an ordinary laborer."

For many days the father tried to convince his son not to leave. "How could you leave your old father all alone?" he protested.

But the son did not give in to his father's arguments, and the old man finally allowed him to go out into the world to learn a trade.

The boy set out. In his travels he came upon a lake. While walking beside the lake, he met a man in a green robe. As you may know, green is the color associated with magic.

The man in the strange attire asked him where he was going, and the boy answered, "I'm going out into the world to find a master from whom I can learn a trade."

"Whenever you feel like it, you may come to me to learn a trade," the man in the green robe said.

The boy was happy that he had found someone willing to teach him. He could hardly wait to go with him, and his eagerness to learn pleased the stranger.

As they were walking beside the lake, the master suddenly jumped into the water and began swimming. "Come jump into the water too, and learn how to swim," he called to the boy.

"I don't dare," the boy answered. "I don't know how to swim. I'm afraid I might drown."

"Don't be afraid," replied the master. "Just jump!"

The boy jumped into the water and began swimming side by side with the green-robed man. When they were in the middle of the lake, the man grabbed the boy by the neck and took him down to the bottom. The stranger was really a devil. He brought the boy to his palace and handed him over to an old woman. Her task was to teach him to be evil. After he had learned the black arts, he would return again to the world above to cause trouble.

The devil went away, and the old woman remained alone with the boy. "My son," she said, "you think that this man is a master, like the master craftsmen on earth above us. Well, he isn't. He's a devil. He tricked me and dragged me here from the other world, and I am a Christian soul. Obey me, and I will help you. I'll teach you his trade. But whenever he comes and asks if you have learned anything, always tell him that you've learned nothing if you want to free yourself of him and return again to earth."

The old woman did as she had promised.

After a while, the devil came and asked the boy, "What have you learned?"

The boy answered, "I still haven't learned anything."

Three years passed in this manner. Whenever the master asked what the boy had learned, he would always answer that he had learned nothing.

Finally, the devil asked him once again, "Have you learned anything?"

Again, the boy answered, "Nothing, and I've even forgotten what I knew before."

His words made the devil angry. "Because you have learned nothing up to now, you will never have the chance to learn anything," he said. "Disappear without a trace. Go wherever your eyes lead you and wherever your legs carry you."

The boy, who had already learned the devil's trade well, jumped into the water and began swimming toward shore. Once he had reached earth, he got out onto the shore and went to his father.

When his father saw him, he ran out to meet him joyfully.

"Where have you been, son, for goodness sake?" he asked.

"I've learned a trade," his son replied, but he would not tell his father anything else. He kept his adventures in the devil's kingdom a secret.

After a while, the people of a neighboring village decided to have a fair.

"Father, let's go to the fair," the son said.

"How can we go?" the father asked. "We have nothing at all to sell there."

"Don't worry about that," the boy reassured him.

The father thought the trip would be a waste of time. But he finally agreed to go in order to please his son, and they set out for the fair.

On the way, the son said to his father, "When we are near the fairground, I'll turn into a fine horse, whose equal can be found nowhere on earth. All of the people at the fair will marvel at me. My master will come to buy a horse. He'll pay whatever price you ask, but whatever you do, don't give him the halter. When you receive the money, remove the halter from the horse's head immediately and strike the ground with it."

When they arrived at the fair, the boy changed into a raven-black horse, equal to none. The old man led the horse about the fair, and all of the people there gathered around him. They stood looking at one another because no one dared ask how much such a fine horse cost.

Then the boy's master came. He had disguised himself as a Turk and had wrapped a turban around his head. His robe reached to the ground.

As soon as he arrived, he said, "I want to buy that horse. Tell me, old man, how much is it?"

The Turk offered whatever amount of money the boy's father requested. Whenever the father raised the price of the horse, more coins appeared in the Turk's hand until they overflowed onto the ground.

When the old man had received the money, he removed the halter from the horse and struck the ground with it. After he had done so, horse and buyer disappeared.

The old man was very worried about his son's disappearance. He had lost him for three years while he was away learning a trade, and he did not want to lose him again.

When his son had returned home from his apprenticeship, the old man had hoped that he would never leave again.

However, all his worrying was unnecessary, for when he reached home with the money, he found his son sitting at the table eating dinner as if nothing extraordinary had happened. The boy refused to say a word about what had taken place.

After a while, another fair was held in front of the tsar's palace. "Let's go to the fair, Father," the son proposed again.

This time the father did not question his boy's judgment, but agreed right away to go with him.

As they approached the fairground, the son said to his father, "Now I'll turn into a shop, a booth full of fine, rich goods, the likes of which have never been seen at the fair. No one there will be able to buy the beautiful things in the shop, but my master will come. He'll pay whatever you ask. Whatever you do, don't give him the keys to the shop. When you have received the money, strike the ground with the keys."

As soon as the boy had turned into a shop full of fine wares, the people at the fair began to marvel.

Along came the master, disguised as a Turk, as he had been before. "How much do you want for everything in the shop?" he asked the old man.

However much the old man overpriced his wares, the Turk agreed to pay. He paid the final sum without a word of protest.

When the old man had received the money, he struck the ground with the keys. At that moment, shop and buyer disappeared.

The shop turned into a pigeon, and the Turk turned into a hawk. The old man watched in fear as the hawk began chasing the pigeon.

While they were chasing each other here and there, the tsar's daughter walked out in front of the palace and began watching. At that moment the pigeon lighted like an arrow onto the girl's hand and became a ring on her finger.

The hawk fell to the earth and turned into a man. He went to the tsar and offered to serve him. The tsar, who had no idea that the man was really the devil in disguise, accepted his offer to serve him for three years. According to their agreement, during that time the devil, disguised as a servant, would want for nothing in the world, neither food, nor drink, nor clothing. At the end of three years, as a reward for his faithful service, the devil was to receive the ring that was on the finger of the tsar's daughter.

While the wicked servant was serving the tsar, the girl was wearing the ring. It became very dear to her. Although it was a ring during the day, at night it turned into a handsome young man, whose companionship made her happy.

"When the time comes for your father to take me from you, don't give me into anyone's hand," the young man instructed her. "Instead, strike me against the ground."

After three years had passed, the tsar went to his daughter and asked her to give him the ring. She threw it onto the ground as if she were angry.

The ring broke, and several small millet seeds appeared in its place. One seed rolled under the tsar's boot. At that moment the devil, disguised as a servant, turned into a sparrow and hastily began pecking at the millet seeds.

The Devil and His Apprentice

After he had pecked up all the grain, he put his beak under the tsar's boot to get the last seed, but suddenly the grain became a sleek cat that seized the sparrow by the neck. And that was the end of the devil!

The cat turned into a handsome young man as the amazed tsar looked on. The young man explained to the puzzled ruler everything that had happened.

The beautiful tsarevna had fallen in love with the young man. Because the tsar was fond of his daughter and wanted her to be happy, he agreed to their marriage.

The young man's father was invited to live in the palace with his son, and everyone lived happily ever after. ❀

Baldy

(Yugoslavia—Serbia)

There once was a tsar who had three daughters. The two oldest girls married the sons of two neighboring tsars and made their father very proud of them. But he decided to leave his kingdom to his youngest daughter because she was the most beautiful and kindest of them all.

The tsar had a servant who was called Baldy because there was not a hair on top of his head. Baldy did nothing except for the gardening, but the garden always looked as if ten people had been working on it. Everyone marveled at its beauty.

The tsar's daughter often looked out the window at the garden and said to herself, "What a lovely garden it is! How neatly it is arranged. It's hard to believe that one little man does it all himself. Why, he can't even be considered a real man. He's just a little mouse of a man."

One morning while looking out the window and daydreaming, the tsar's daughter caught sight of Baldy. "For goodness sake, Baldy," she said, "how can you plant and maintain such a large garden all by yourself?"

"My lady, if you want to know, get up early, and you'll see," he replied.

The tsar's daughter told her parents nothing about what Baldy had said. The next morning, she got up very early and looked out at the garden. Baldy was standing there alone.

Suddenly, a winged horse, strong as a dragon, flew up to Baldy. It brought him a warrior's suit of clothing and weapons. Three or four people were sitting on its back, and they did the gardening for Baldy.

Baldy put on the clothes, and he became a completely different person. He was no longer bald, but as handsome as a young man could possibly be. He rode around the garden on his dragon horse, and it began breathing fire. Sparks flashed from its nostrils.

When the tsar's daughter saw Baldy as a handsome young man, she fell in love with him. She did not tell anyone about it for a long time. Finally, after many suitors began coming to her father asking for her hand in marriage, she said that she did not want to marry anyone but Baldy.

The tsar and tsaritsa scolded their daughter. "How could you marry a servant? Even if he were a handsome, strong servant, it would be unthinkable, let alone a gap-toothed old man like Baldy. Do you want to bring disgrace upon the family?"

The tsar's beautiful daughter would not listen to her parents. "Either I marry Baldy," she said, "or I won't marry at all."

When her father saw that she was determined, he dressed her in beggar's clothing and took away her royal title. She gave up her right to inherit her father's kingdom so that she could marry the gardener.

The tsar gave them a little plot of land outside of town as a wedding gift. Baldy planted a garden there and built a little cottage. He began living with the tsarevna as if he were an ordinary gardener, taking his vegetables to town and selling them in order to earn his daily bread.

Whenever he wanted to, though, he could turn into a handsome young man. He had only to whistle, and the dragon horse would gallop up to him bringing clothes and shining weapons befitting a gentleman.

The tsarevna loved him dearly and never complained about having to leave her magnificent palace to live in poverty.

And so life went on for some time, but suddenly enemies attacked Baldy's father-in-law on both sides of his kingdom. The tsar did not know what to do.

"I can hope for help from the husbands of my two daughter who married tsars," he said, "but the daughter in whom I had placed my highest hopes is married to a good-for-nothing."

Greatly worried, the tsar issued a command for everyone who could put on a sword to join the army. Soldiers, one after another, constantly marched against the enemy, but bad news kept reaching the tsar's ears—his armies were defeated.

Finally, the tsar himself went to see what was happening. Small and great warriors marched behind him, and even Baldy rode behind him on a little horse.

Everyone laughed at Baldy. "Now everything will be all right," they said mockingly. "Baldy's going. He'll destroy the enemy and bring peace to the land."

When the enemy was in sight, they set up camp, and Baldy pitched a tent for himself. They remained there for three days. Nothing happened.

On the fourth day, the battle began. Baldy gave a whistle, and his dragon horse twirled around before him. He put on the fine clothing that the horse had brought, took up his sword, mounted his horse, and flew into battle.

As soon as he began fighting, the enemy became confused. It was impossible to decide who was killing more of the enemy's soldiers, whether Baldy was hacking more of them down with his sword or his horse was trampling more of them under his hooves. In a matter of minutes, the enemy forces split up and ran helter-skelter.

The news reached the tsar in his tent that among his warriors was a hero who had defeated the enemy and that now his foe was begging to establish peace.

The tsar commanded that the hero come before him to ask for whatever he wanted as his reward. Before the first messengers had left to seek out the hero, however, other messengers came to the tsar and told him that the wonderful warrior was none other than Baldy.

The tsar was amazed when he heard this news. He refused to believe it. "How could that be? If it had been Baldy, he certainly would have come to me. No, no, you must be mistaken."

Baldy sent word to him. "On the way home, I'll ride by your side," he wrote.

The tsar read Baldy's message, then forgot about him for the time being. His mind was preoccupied with drawing up a peace treaty that would be advantageous to himself and his subjects.

After peace was established and they were on their way home, Baldy rolled up his tent, gathered his few belongings, and put them onto his little horse. Then he gave a whistle, and the dragon horse twirled around and around before him. He put on his fine clothing, mounted the horse, and rode beside the tsar so that everyone could see that it was he who had defeated the enemy.

When the tsar recognized that the young man was indeed his old gardener, Baldy, he wept with joy. He arrived home in great happiness and begged his daughter's forgiveness for not trusting her judgment.

Then the tsar handed over his kingdom to Baldy and lived to see Baldy rule the land. ❖

The Magic Dagger

(Yugoslavia—Serbia)

*O*nce upon a time an ambitious young man named Stefan made a vow that he would marry none other than the tsar's daughter. His family tried to discourage him because they considered his desire a foolish dream. After all, he was poor and could hardly hope to compete with tsareviches, the sons of tsars, who came daily to woo the beautiful tsarevna.

One day Stefan went to the tsar and asked for his daughter's hand in marriage.

The kindly tsar, not wanting to hurt the feelings of such a resolute young man by refusing him outright, said, "All right, son, I'll give you my daughter if within eight days you can bring back my three favorite horses. They were stolen by the evil *vilas* who live on Vila Mountain.

"The first horse is pure white, without a spot on him. He was born mysteriously, without a mother or father.

"The second horse is red with a black head. He has never been ridden by anyone.

"The third horse is raven black with a white head and white legs. He has never worn horseshoes because he won't let a blacksmith near him.

"If you load the horses down with as much treasure as they can carry and bring them back to me and my wife, the tsaritsa, you may marry our daughter. But if you aren't able to accomplish the task, my daughter will not be yours."

The strange command puzzled the young man. However, he thanked the tsar politely and went home, trusting in God to give him the help he needed.

Fortunately, while Stefan was speaking with the tsar, the tsar's daughter was listening to everything and was peeking from behind the door at the courageous young man, who seemed to her the most handsome and the nicest person in the world. She decided without any hesitation that she loved him and that it was her destiny to marry him.

Of course, destiny sometimes needs a hand in such matters, so the tsarevna wrote a letter and sent it to the young man via her most trusted servant. In it she wrote that the next morning he should come to her secretly and that he should do exactly as she said if he wished to marry her.

The tsarevna knew that in her father's armory was a dagger with magic powers. That night, after she sent off the message, she took the magic dagger secretly from her father's collection of weapons. It was beautifully ornate, and whoever looked at it fell under the spell of its hypnotic beauty. The most evil of men and women became good, and the wildest of beasts became docile after looking at its shining blade.

The next morning the tsarevna met Stefan, who came just as she had advised. They talked and agreed that they were very much in love. They swore that nothing other than the grave would ever separate them.

Then the tsar's daughter said, "Here is my horse. Mount him and take the road eastward to Vila Mountain, where the evil spirits live. When you come to a mountain with three peaks, turn to the left until you come upon a meadow of pearls where wild horses are grazing.

"Select the three horses that my father told you about. If they should become frightened, take out this dagger and turn the blade toward the sun so that the meadow becomes bright with light. All the horses will come to you of their own accord and kneel before you like lambs. You'll be able to catch them easily.

"After you have selected the horses, look around and you'll see a tree in the middle of the meadow. Its roots are copper, its branches are silver, and its foliage is gold. Go up to it and strike the sheath of the dagger on the root. The tree will open up and golden coins will fall out. Take them and load them onto the three horses.

"Then gallop back here with them as fast as you can before the *vilas* see you. If those wicked spirits catch you, they'll tear you apart and leave your bones to bleach in the sun. When Father sees his three favorite horses again, he'll be so happy that he'll let me marry you."

Stefan listened to her words and took heart, although he was a little worried about meeting the *vilas*. He mounted the tsarevna's horse, put the magic dagger in his belt, and set out directly for Vila Mountain.

When he came to the mountain with three peaks, he saw a meadow of pearls with grazing horses. The horses became frightened and ran madly in all directions, whinnying.

Stefan was afraid that their commotion would alert the *vilas* to his presence. He took out the magic dagger and turned the blade toward the sun. The sun's rays were reflected in the dagger so that the sun seemed to be rising over the mountain, and the entire meadow became bright.

The glittering blade hypnotized the horses. They calmed down and came up to him meekly. As they came, they kneeled on their front legs before him. He selected the three horses that belonged to the tsar.

When he had chosen the horses, he looked around and caught sight of a tree in the middle of the meadow. He went up to it, knocked at the root with the sheath of his dagger, and the tree opened up. Golden coins came spilling forth. He filled several sacks and loaded the coins onto the three horses.

Everything had gone smoothly, but suddenly three *vilas* ran out of the forest into the meadow. They were beautiful women with golden, flowing hair, but their eyes gleamed wickedly. They waved their hands wildly like mad women.

"We're going to tear you from limb to limb!" they shrieked as they rushed at him. "How dare you trespass on our mountain!"

Stefan froze. He looked at their merciless eyes. Then he thought of the beautiful tsarevna waiting for him.

After a moment's hesitation, the young man quickly held the blade of his magic dagger toward the sun. The wild eyes of the *vilas* suddenly were filled with peace and love. They smiled at Stefan, who immediately took advantage of their changed dispositions and set out for the palace at full speed.

When Stefan came before the tsar and showed him the horses and the coins, the tsar was amazed. He could do nothing other than give the young man his daughter in marriage as he had promised. And because he was a kind, honorable tsar who always kept his word, he did not delay in setting the wedding date.

He asked Stefan what he expected to receive as a dowry from the tsarevna.

"Your majesty," the young man answered, "I don't want money or jewels. I already have my heart's desire. I have your daughter. The only other wish I have is to possess the magic dagger as my reward."

The tsar laughed and gave him the dagger gladly. Singing a merry song, Stefan returned with his new bride and the magic dagger to his humble home, where he and the tsarevna lived happily ever after. ✿

You Reap What You Sow

(Yugoslavia—Serbia)

*O*nce upon a time there was a girl named Cveta who had a wicked stepmother. The stepmother had an ugly daughter of her own, whom she loved dearly. However, she hated her beautiful stepdaughter. She and her own daughter slapped the girl, scolded her all the time, and tormented her with hunger and poverty in the hope that someday she would simply die so that they would not have to put up with her.

The worse they treated her, however, the healthier and prettier Cveta became. The wicked stepmother saw that she would not be rid of her very easily, so one day when the girl's father had gone to market and was not there to protect her, she drove Cveta out of the house.

"Get out, and don't come back!" the stepmother screamed at Cveta in a shrill voice.

The unwanted stepdaughter walked down the road, not knowing where to go. Finally, she went into the deep forest and wandered here and there in search of a way out until she saw a fire burning in the distance. She went in the direction from which the firelight shone.

She came upon a little cottage and went inside. The cottage was dirty and in bad need of cleaning and straightening. The fire that she had seen burning while she was still far away in the forest was scattered about the hearth and dying out.

Cveta took a broom and cleaned the cottage nicely. She put out the fire, carried in more wood, and started a fresh fire. Then, she sat and waited for the owner of the little cottage to come home.

In the evening, the wind began blowing so hard that the trees snapped as if they had been pulled up at the roots. Shaking with fear, the frightened Cveta hid behind the stove.

Soon a scaly dragoness with enormous wings came flying up. She entered the cottage and began to sniff around. "A spirit sent from heaven is here," she said in a voice surprisingly soft for a dragoness. "Come out, heavenly spirit. I won't harm you."

The trembling girl came out from behind the stove hesitantly. Then the dragoness asked, "Did you clean my cottage and light my fire?"

"I did," Cveta answered.

"Good," said the dragoness. "Now please search in my scales and see if I have any fleas or bugs in my head."

Cveta saw that the dragoness was not the fierce and fiery sort, so she sat down and let her place her head on her lap. Then she began looking for fleas among the scales. To her dismay, she found that the creature's head was full of maggots and smelled like a bug.

"Does my head smell bad, girl?" asked the dragoness.

Cveta did not want to hurt her feelings, so she replied, "No, it doesn't smell bad. It smells just like a bouquet of dried flowers."

Early the next morning, the dragoness went off into the forest. Before leaving, she ordered the girl to feed her animals and to have supper ready for her when she came home in the evening.

Cveta began calling the animals together. She expected a few cows and some hens and geese to come running at her call. She was amazed when, instead, a frolicking group of owls, ravens, wolves, foxes, badgers, and skunks came dashing out of the forest. Every kind of wild animal imaginable came to be fed. Cveta fed them kindly and even gave the wolf a pat on its furry back. Then, the animals went their separate ways and disappeared into the dark forest.

When the dragoness came home in the evening, she asked whether her animals had been fed.

"They have," the girl answered.

After Cveta had worked at the cottage for several days, the dragoness took her into a room filled with chests of various colors and shapes. Some were gilded with gold. Others were decorated with jewels. Still others had plain wood veneers. Some were so heavy that they could not be lifted, and others were so small and light that they could be held in a person's hand.

"If you want, you may go home now," the dragoness said. "Because you have served me so well, you may choose whichever of these chests you like and take it home with you as your reward for helping me so faithfully."

Cveta chose a small, plain chest that could be held in her hand.

"Why have you taken the most ordinary chest?" the dragoness asked.

"Because I know that the least is in it," Cveta answered. "In the few days that I've been with you, I haven't earned any more than the chest contains."

The unwanted stepdaughter reluctantly started out for home. She was sorry to leave the dragoness that had been kind to her.

When Cveta arrived home with the chest and opened it, she found that it was filled to the brim with golden coins. Her stepmother was impressed.

After listening to the story of her stepdaughter's adventures, she sent her own daughter into the forest to visit the dragoness and to bring back a chest full of golden coins, too.

The nasty-tempered girl came upon the same cottage in the depths of the forest, but she did not want to touch the dirty ashes of the dying fire, let alone fix a new one. She was far too lazy to sweep the cottage, so she searched for a comfortable nook and fell asleep.

When the dragoness came home in the evening, the wind blew just as the stepsister had warned. The girl was not afraid because she already knew that she would not be hurt.

"Heavenly spirit, why haven't you touched my fire or cleaned my cottage?" the dragoness asked.

The unpleasant girl answered rudely, "I don't clean my own cottage. Mother and Sister do it for me, so why should I clean yours?"

"All right, never mind," said the dragoness. "Please search my scales, and see if there are any fleas or bugs in my head."

The girl peeped into the scales on the dragoness's head and began spitting. "Pppht! What a stench! I can't stand being near you."

"All right, never mind," the dragoness said again.

The next day the dragoness went away into the forest and ordered the girl to feed her animals, as her sister had done.

When the girl saw that the animals were wild, she took up a club and began screaming. She hit the fox in the leg and the wolf on the head, and then she broke the birds' wings. Finally, she drove all of the animals away.

When the dragoness came home in the evening, she asked the girl if she had fed the animals.

"Feed them, indeed! What kind of devils are they anyway? I fed them alright, with a club—like this!" she said, twirling the heavy club wildly in the air to show what she had done.

"All right, never mind then," the dragoness sighed sadly.

When morning came, she told the girl to go home. "You have served me long enough," she said. "Choose whichever one of these chests you would like and take it home with you."

The girl was delighted to think that she did not have to stay with the dragoness as many days as Cveta had. That's what comes of showing the old bag of scales who's boss, she thought to herself.

In her greed, she chose the heaviest chest, which was gilded with gold and decorated with jewel-encrusted designs. She nearly broke her back dragging it home. For the first time in her life, she worked so hard that she began to sweat.

When she reached home, she and the stepmother quickly opened the beautiful chest to see the great wealth inside. Two terrible green snakes jumped out of it. One bit the mother in the eyes, and the other struck her daughter's eyes. The dreadful snakes drank the eyes out of the heads of the two evil women, and they had to go about blind for the rest of their lives.

Cveta, the beautiful stepdaughter who had been treated so cruelly, became known throughout the country for her beauty and kindness. A handsome, gentle tsar heard about her goodness and married her.

However, she did not abandon her evil stepmother and stepsister. Instead, she took them and her father to live in the palace with her, where they were well taken care of until the end of their days here on earth. ✿

The Shepherd and the Three Vilas

(Macedonia)

One morning while watching over his sheep in a forest glen near a swift-flowing river, a young shepherd saw three beautiful maidens swimming in the water.

They were so beautiful that the shepherd could not take his eyes off them. Oh, if only I were closer to the river, he thought, I'd grab one of those beautiful girls by the hand and convince her to marry me.

The girls came out onto the riverbank and got dressed. Then they took a shortcut through the forest and disappeared before the shepherd's very eyes.

Early the next morning, the shepherd drove his sheep to the same spot and hid in a small clump of trees so that he could watch the girls again while they were swimming.

As soon as the sun rose, the three girls came. The shepherd was not able to grab one by the hand that morning either. He was too far away from them again.

On the third day the shepherd hid in a bush that was close to the river and waited for the girls. When the sun rose, they walked up smiling, as merry as bright stars. They took off their dresses and went into the river to swim.

The shepherd sat and thought about how he might approach one of them. He thought that he might be able to grab one by the hand if he took away their dresses so that they would have nothing to wear except the slips they were swimming in. If they came to him and asked for their dresses back, then he might be able to make their acquaintance.

Having mulled over this plan, the shepherd decided that it just might work. He ran over and grabbed the dresses.

When the girls saw what had happened, they were astonished. They stopped swimming in the middle of the river and began begging the shepherd to return their dresses to them. In exchange for their dresses, they promised to do him a favor.

The shepherd was certain that he could coax one of them to marry him. "I'll give you your dresses, girls," he said to them, "if one of you will marry me. Otherwise, I won't give them to you. Instead, I'll make a fire and burn them so that you'll have to walk home in your slips."

The girls were horrified. How could they walk down the road wearing only their slips? Everyone would be shocked.

"Very well, young man," said the oldest girl. "You want one of us to be your wife, but you should know beforehand that we are not three ordinary sisters. We are *vilas*. As you know, *vilas* are spirits with magical powers. Therefore, you mustn't marry one of us, or else everyone will laugh at you for having a *vila* for a wife."

"I don't care. Even if you are wicked *vilas*, I still want to marry one of you. I won't give back your dresses until you agree," the young man told them.

When the sisters heard his words, they were convinced that they would not get their dresses back until one of them agreed to marry him.

"If that's the way it has to be, take whichever one of us you want, young man," they said, "but give us our dresses so that we can go home, for we live very far away."

The shepherd was delighted. He looked at the *vilas* and tried to decide which one he would choose. All three sisters were extremely beautiful. But, finally he asked for the youngest because she seemed gentle and kind. The two older sisters agreed that he should have the youngest *vila* for his wife.

Then, they called him aside and told him never to give the little *vila* her dress because it contained magic powers. She would run away if she put it on. They advised him to give her another dress to wear.

The shepherd did as the two *vilas* said. He gave them their dresses, and they hurried home. He kept the dress of the youngest sister, and she went home with the shepherd wearing his long shirt.

The young man dressed her in a bridal gown and married her. No one laughed at him for having a *vila* for a wife, for she was the most beautiful woman in the village.

The shepherd and the *vila* lived together happily for almost a year. The *vila* was a good wife, loving and industrious.

Then one day they were invited to attend the wedding of the shepherd's cousin. At the wedding celebration, the young women started a round dance called the *kolo*. Only the shepherd's wife did not join in. She could not dance the *kolo* because she did not have her *vila's* dress. Her dress contained the power that enabled her to dance gracefully.

Vilas are famed for their ability to dance. They are light on their feet and flit about like stars on a frosty night. The women, who had never seen a *vila* dance before, wanted the shepherd's wife to join in. They pleaded with him to let his wife wear her *vila's* dress just this one time.

Because of the insistent pleading of the women and girls, the shepherd finally agreed. He went home, took the dress from its hiding place, and brought it to the wedding celebration. Before giving the dress to his wife, however, the shepherd closed the windows and doors so that she would not be able to escape. Then the *vila* put on the dress.

When she joined in and began dancing the *kolo*, everyone at the gathering admired her. They watched her movements as if enchanted.

The dance ended, and the *vila* went up to her husband. "Good-bye, my dear," she said. "The magic powers in my dress have me under a spell. I must obey them and leave you now." Then she flew up the chimney and disappeared.

When the shepherd saw that his wife was running away, he shouted after her, "Wife, wife, why are you doing this to me? Why are you running away from me up the chimney? I beg of you, dear wife, tell me where to search for you so that I can see you once again."

"Search for me, dear," the *vila* called down the chimney, "in the village of Kuškundaljevo. You will find me there." Then she flew away into the clouds.

Several days later the shepherd set out on a long journey to find the village of Kuškundaljevo. He passed through many villages and towns and cities. At each place he asked where Kuškundaljevo was located. Everyone who heard the shepherd speak the name of the village knew nothing about it. Even people who took pride in their knowledge of geography had never heard of Kuškundaljevo.

After he had gone through all the villages and towns and cities of Macedonia in search of his wife, he traveled through the mountains.

While crossing the second mountain, he came upon an old man who stood leaning against a beech tree with a staff in his hands.

"Young man, why are you wandering in this wilderness where the cock doesn't crow and where human feet have never tread?" the old man asked the shepherd.

"Misfortune compels me to walk here, uncle," the shepherd replied. "I am going to ask you something. If you know the answer, please tell me. Is there perhaps a village in this wilderness by the name of Kuškundaljevo?

"I have never heard of it, young man, although I have been living here 200 years. Why are you searching for it?"

"One year ago, while I was watching my sheep beside a river, I noticed three sisters swimming in the water," answered the shepherd. "They were *vilas*. On the third morning, I took away their dresses. They gave me the youngest sister to be my wife in exchange for their dresses.

"The two older sisters warned me not to give my wife her dress or she would run away from me because of the magic powers in it. I believed them, uncle, and kept the dress hidden until recently.

"Then, the women of the village convinced me to give it to her so that she could dance the *kolo* at my cousin's wedding. I closed all the doors so that she couldn't run away, but I forgot to close the chimney vent.

"At the end of the dance, she flew up the chimney. And when I asked her where I should look for her, she told me to search in the village of Kuškundaljevo.

"There you have it. That's my misfortune, uncle. Now, if you know anything at all, please tell me."

"I don't recognize the name of the village, young man. If you travel on for another month, you'll find another old man like me. Give him my regards. He is my brother, who is 300 years old and wiser than I. He is Tsar of the Animals. Perhaps he can tell you something about the village." Then the old man bade the shepherd farewell.

After the shepherd had traveled for another month, he came upon another old man, sitting near a well. He greeted him. Then he related his story to the Tsar of the Animals, just as he had told it to his younger brother.

"Wait here for a while, young man," said the Tsar of the Animals. "I will call the animals and ask them about the village you are searching for."

The old man sent a command to all the animals to come before him. After a while, they arrived. The Tsar of the Animals addressed them. "Lions, bears, wolves, foxes—everyone—listen to what I am about to ask. Every day you walk past villages and towns in your travels, and you know much that is unknown to man. Have you ever heard of a village called Kuškundaljevo?

"We haven't, honorable tsar. We've never heard that name before," the animals answered, all at the same time.

"You see, young man, there is no village by that name. But don't give up. Travel on for another month, and you'll find my other brother. He is Tsar of the Birds, and he knows every bird that flies above the clouds. Perhaps the birds have heard of the village you are looking for."

The shepherd sadly went on his way. After another month had passed, he came to the third brother, Tsar of the Birds. He greeted the tsar and told him that his brothers sent their regards. Then, he related his own story of misfortune from beginning to end.

The old man sent word immediately to his eagles and ravens and to the rest of the birds to come to him. Within twenty-four hours, all the birds in the world had flown to the tsar and were waiting for his command.

"Listen to me, eagles, ravens, and every bird on earth," he said. "Has any one of you heard of the village called Kuškundaljevo?"

"We've never heard that name until now, honorable tsar," the birds told him.

"Well, such a village must not exist, young man, because no one has heard of it, neither the gray eagle, nor the other birds. I am 400 years old, and I've never heard of it," the old man told him.

At that moment a lame magpie approached the tsar. As soon as he saw her, the tsar asked, "Why are you late, magpie? You're the last to come to me."

"I am late, honorable tsar, first because I am lame and second because I live very far away, right near Kuškundaljevo, where the *vilas* live. When your message reached me, I was helping the *vilas* harvest *immortelle*, the flower that never dies. While I was threshing, a clumsy *vila* hit me in the leg, and because of the pain, I couldn't fly fast enough to get here on time," the magpie told the tsar.

"Young man, did you hear what the magpie said?" the old man asked the youth. "She is from the village you're looking for. Get ready if you want to go there with her. I'll give you an eagle to ride. Just mount him, and he'll take you right to Kuškundaljevo."

"If you will do me that kindness, honorable tsar," said the shepherd, "I will never forget you."

Then the Tsar of the Birds ordered one of the largest eagles to take the shepherd to Kuškundaljevo. The magpie went on ahead, and the eagle followed her.

They arrived at the village early in the morning. On the outskirts, the shepherd got off the eagle's back and went to the first house to ask where the three *vilas* lived. Fortunately, it was the very house he was looking for, so he searched no further.

As soon as he entered the yard, the two older sisters saw him. They felt sorry for him because he looked so sad and tired.

"What a shame! Our poor brother-in-law has walked all over Macedonia in search of his unfaithful wife," said the oldest sister. "Because he has suffered so much, we should help him by tying our youngest sister to the flying saddle so that he can take her home." The middle sister agreed.

They went outside and welcomed their brother-in-law warmly. Then, they asked him why he had given his wife her dress and how she had managed to run away. He told them about his long journey to their village, and he begged them to return his wife.

"Don't worry, brother-in-law," they told him. "We're on your side. We'll tie her to the flying saddle, and you will sit on it. You'll have to fly quickly to cross the three mountains that you passed to get here. When you have crossed them, you have nothing more to worry about.

"Now go into the house so that we can tie your wife to the saddle while she's asleep. Then, you'll climb onto it.

"As you are running away she will wake up and scream as loud as she can, so that her magic horse can hear her. It will come running to save her. If the horse catches up to you when you have already crossed the three mountains, it can do nothing to you. But if it catches you over the first two mountains or in front of the last mountain, it will cut you to pieces and take away your wife."

The *vilas* tied their sister to the flying saddle and the shepherd mounted it. The winds lifted the saddle into the air.

When the young man was close to the first of the three mountains, his *vila* wife awoke and cried out to summon help. As soon as her faithful horse heard her screams, it flew after the shepherd.

Swift as lightning, the *vila*'s white horse pursued its mistress. As they crossed the first mountain, the menacing horse came so close that the shepherd could see its razor-sharp teeth, clacking like scissors ready to tear him to shreds.

As the flying saddle leaped over the second mountain, the horse locked its teeth around it. The shepherd's heart gave a leap, but he dashed on desperately as his *vila* wife laughed madly.

The saddle began to slow down when they came to the third mountain. The horse had bitten a large chunk out of it. Its terrible teeth were poised to clamp down on the shepherd's head, but it was too late. The flying saddle carried the shepherd and his wife across the last mountain. The white horse turned back, for its power did not reach beyond that point.

The shepherd returned home with the *vila*. He immediately burned her dress so that she could never return to Kuškundaljevo.

After the flames had licked up the last fragments of the material, his *vila* wife sighed. She explained that the magic powers in the dress had ruled her soul. When she was wearing the dress, she was quite a different person. Its magic powers made her wild and untamable, rather than gentle and kind. She was glad that the dress would never be able to influence her again.

As for the shepherd, he lived happily ever after with his *vila* wife. Several very beautiful daughters were born to them. And to the daughters were born even more beautiful daughters, who were said to be the most beautiful girls in the world. ❁

Three Eels

(Yugoslavia—Serbia)

There once lived a fisherman. He went fishing with a net every day, and for three days in a row he caught only one eel per day. When he caught the third eel on the third day, he grumbled, "What a terrible catch! Imagine, only one eel a day!"

Suddenly one of the eels started speaking in a human voice. "Why are you complaining, foolish man? You have happened upon great good fortune. Kill any one of us eels and cut him into four parts. Give one part to your wife to eat, the second to your dog, the third to your mare, and bury the fourth behind your house.

"If you do as I say, your wife will bear twin boys, the dog will bear two pups, and the mare will give birth to two colts. Moreover, two sabers will grow from the earth behind your house."

The fisherman followed the eel's instructions, and everything happened just as the eel had promised. The fortunate man became richer by two sons, two dogs, two colts, and two sabers.

Time passed, and the sons grew up. One day one of them said, "Father, I see that you are poor and can't feed us. Let me take one of the horses, one of the dogs, and a saber. I'll go into the wide world in search of my destiny."

The young man turned to his brother and added these words. "Good-bye, brother. Guard the house, and take care of the farm. Give Father the respect he deserves while I am gone.

"Here is a bottle of water. Keep it with you always. If the water turns cloudy, you'll know I have perished."

Having uttered these words, he set out on his journey. He traveled until he came to a large town. As he rode past the palace, the tsar's daughter happened to be looking out the window. When she caught sight of him, she fell head over heels in love with him. It was love at first sight.

The tsarevna asked her father to invite the young man into the palace. When the young man entered, the tsarevna looked at him attentively. She noticed that he had a saber, a dog, and a horse—all the equipment that young men should have. She fell even more deeply in love with him and said to her father, "I wish to marry this young man."

The tsar, who loved his daughter dearly, agreed to her request. The young man, too, was not against it. The wedding was arranged, and the couple was married.

One evening the young man was standing with his wife by the palace window. He saw a great mountain enveloped in flames in the distance. "What is burning over there?" he asked.

"Don't ask, my lord. It is a dreadful mountain. During the daytime it shines, and at night it burns. Whoever climbs the mountain is cursed and turns to stone right on the spot."

The young man decided to investigate the strange mountain. His wife objected. "Don't go there, please," she begged. "It is very dangerous."

He paid no attention to his wife's protests. Instead, he put on his saber, called his faithful dog, and headed out in the direction of the mountain.

As he approached the mountain, he noticed a sorceress sitting on a cliff. She was holding a staff in one hand and some kind of herb in the other.

The young man shouted to her. "Tell me, why is this mountain so very strange and different from the other mountains?"

"Come closer, and you'll find out," the sorceress answered.

She led him into a courtyard surrounded by a fence made from the bones of the young men who had lost their lives there. In the middle of the courtyard stood the statues of people who had been turned to stone. No sooner had the youth entered the yard of the sorceress than he, his horse, and his dog were turned to stone.

At that moment the water in the bottle he had left with his brother became muddy. His brother called to their parents. "Come quickly, Mother and Father. The water in the bottle is muddy. My brother has perished. I must go in search of him. Give me your blessing."

The old couple grieved, but they knew their son had no choice but to search for his twin brother. They gave him their blessing, and he set out.

He went from village to village, from town to town, until good fortune led him to the very town and the very palace where his brother had lived.

When the tsar caught sight of him, he ran to his daughter and asked for a reward for being the bearer of glad tidings. "See, your husband is here," he cried.

The tsarevna ran out and looked at her brother-in-law. The twin brothers resembled one another like two peas in a pod. She threw her arms around his neck, taking him to be her husband.

The tsar had already decided that the traveler was his son-in-law. The young man, although he was amazed at their caresses, soon figured out that he had been mistaken for his brother. He began acting as if he really were the tsar's son-in-law.

That evening the tsarevna called him to bed. He lay down and placed his saber between himself and the tsarevna. She was amazed by his strange behavior, but he claimed he was not sleepy.

He got up and went over to the window. Noticing the magic mountain, he asked, "Why does that mountain glow so, wife?"

"What's the matter with you? I've already told you what kind of mountain it is."

"What kind of mountain is it?"

"The kind that turns whoever climbs onto it to stone. I was afraid that you had wandered there by accident."

After hearing what the tsarevna said, the young man grew sad. He could barely wait for morning to come. When it dawned, he mounted his horse, put on his saber, called his dog, and set out in the direction of the mountain.

Like his brother, he, too, noticed the sorceress. He grabbed his saber. Without uttering a word, he set his dog on her.

The sorceress was frightened and began begging for mercy. "Please, please, tell your dog to leave me alone."

"Where is my brother?" the young man cried.

The shaken sorceress led his twin to him. He was no longer under the sorceress's spell. She had returned his soul and had given him the gift of speech.

The brothers set out for the palace. On the way, the brother who had been placed under the spell said, "Brother, let's go back and save all the other people who were bewitched by the sorceress. What do you say?"

His twin agreed, and they did just that. They rode back to the mountain to the place where the evil sorceress stood. They grabbed her and tore the magic herbs out of her hand. Then, they ran to the courtyard, where they began rubbing the herbs on the statues of people who had been turned to stone.

The bewitched people came to life and began speaking. Then, the brothers slew the evil sorceress. They returned to the tsar's palace and each person they had brought back to life went his own way. ✿

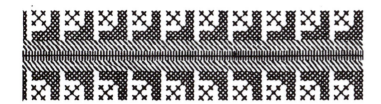

Part IV

TALES OF EVERYDAY LIFE

Ero and the Turk

(Yugoslavia—Serbia)

Note: Ero is a character famous throughout Yugoslavia for his silliness. For instance, once Ero claimed that he had visited heaven and had spoken with the dead. On another occasion, Ero foolishly thanked the tsar for throwing figs in his face. There are many stories about him in Yugoslavia. Here is one.

One day a Turk was busily plowing with a wooden plow and a pair of oxen on a slope near a bridge when Ero came down the road with several packhorses.

As Ero approached, the Turk decided to make fun of him. "Giddap, my dappled ox, giddap!" he shouted. "After all, you have some sense, but Ero has none."

Ero went up to the bridge and drove his horses across, but he did not follow them. He started bellowing at the top of his lungs, "Woe is me! Now what will I do?"

When he heard Ero's cry, the Turk halted the oxen and ran up to him as fast as he could. "What's wrong, Ero? What is it?"

"Woe is me! Lord, have mercy on me. The horses have gone across the bridge, and they've left me here on this side."

"Well, just get going and follow the horses across."

"I don't dare go across for the life of me, sir."

"Just go ahead and don't be so silly!" said the Turk. "Why don't you dare cross the bridge? Everyone else does, including your packhorses."

Foolish Ero would not budge an inch. He just kept howling and wailing.

Finally, the Turk said, "Just what will you give me for carrying you across the bridge on my back?"

"What do you want, sir?"

"Give me twelve *para*, twelve coins."

"All right, let's go!"

The Turk lifted Ero onto his shoulders and carried him across the bridge. When he set him down on the other side, Ero started feeling his pocket frantically.

"Sir, I don't have a single *para*; I swear I don't."

"It can't be true," the amazed Turk replied. "Why are you lying to me, you numskull?" Ero remained silent. "Very well, then, get up onto my back again."

Ero mounted the Turk's shoulders obediently once again, and once again he was carried back across the bridge.

The Turk flung him onto the ground. "Look here, idiot, you can just stay on this side of the river until you croak if you can't pay me."

The Turk went back to his oxen and continued plowing.

Suddenly, Ero jumped up and walked across the bridge. When he reached the other side of the river, he shouted, "Hey, Turk, do you still think that your dappled ox has more sense than I do? Your ox may be smart, but he hasn't ridden horseback across the bridge on you two times as I have." ❁

How the Order Was Obeyed

(Croatia)

*O*nce upon a time Ali-Pasha Rizvanbegović gave an order that no one should walk the streets at night without a lantern. The order seemed foolish to his people, but every good citizen obeyed. Who would dare question the judgment of Ali-Pasha? So no one left home after eight o'clock without carrying a lantern.

One night soon afterward, two guards caught a peaceful citizen walking without a lantern. They stopped the man.

"Don't you know that Ali-Pasha has given an order declaring that no one should walk about at night without a lantern?" one of the guards asked him.

"I know," answered the peaceful citizen.

"Then, where's your lantern?"

"Here it is." The man showed the guard a lantern that he had been holding at his side. The lantern had no candle inside.

"Where's the candle?" asked the guard.

"Nothing was said about a candle. The order simply stated that people should walk at night with a lantern."

The two guards looked at the man in disbelief. Then they looked at each other meaningfully.

They let him go, but told him that it was absolutely necessary to have a candle in the lantern.

The honest citizen promised solemnly that he would not walk about without a candle in his lantern again.

The next evening the guards caught the same man walking around in the dark. "Why are you without a lantern again?" they screamed at him.

"I have a lantern. Here it is," the man hastened to say, and he stuck his lantern in front of the guards' noses.

"And where is the candle?"

"Here is the candle." The man pointed inside his lantern.

"Why didn't you light it, idiot?"

"But sir," the man answered, "nothing was said in the order about lighting the candle."

That is how an ordinary Croatian citizen played the fool to defy the order of the oppressive Turkish official, Ali-Pasha, who was made to look more foolish than his subject. ❁

It's Not Easy to Steal from a Gypsy

(Croatia—Dalmatia)

Note: Romanies (Gypsies), who originated in India, migrated to the southern Balkans before 1300 and were well established there by 1400. They worked as artisans, animal trainers, entertainers, and tinkers. Because they traveled and never settled permanently in one place, people regarded them with suspicion. Frequently, when something went wrong, Romanies were blamed. They became scapegoats, whose existence alternated between periods of acceptance and persecution. Images of Romanies as cunning thieves were common. The following story mocks the unjust stereotype.

A Gypsy once went to Dubrovnik in order to buy some salt. He left his horse in the Gypsy camp tied to a tree while he went into town after the salt.

When he returned, he saw that someone had stolen the halter from his horse and that the horse was wandering around the camp by itself.

The Gypsy had no idea who had stolen the halter, but he began shouting so that everyone would hear him. Soon a crowd had gathered around him.

Waving his arms angrily, he screamed, "Who stole the halter from my horse? Return the horse's halter at once, or pay me for it. If it isn't returned to me this very moment, I swear on my Gypsy's honor that I'll do the first thing that pops into my head!"

What kind of terrible revenge will that be? wondered the people in the camp. Does he plan to slit our throats? Or will he burn down our camp? Or is he thinking about slaughtering our horses? They began trembling because they were afraid that in his anger he would hurt someone.

"Let's look through each other's sacks," they proposed, "so that the innocent won't have to pay for the crime of one guilty man."

The man who had stolen the halter heard this proposal. When he saw a group of Gypsies approaching to search his sacks, he quickly removed the halter from his bag and gave it to the rightful owner.

Then, out of curiosity, he asked, "If the halter had not been found, what had you sworn on your Gypsy's honor to do?"

"On my Gypsy's honor, I would have done nothing except return to town in order to buy a new halter for my horse," answered the smiling Gypsy. ❖

The Aga and the Stable Boy

(Yugoslavia—Kosovo and Metohija)

One day a wealthy *aga* (Turkish official), went to the stable to ask his stable boy to saddle a horse so that he could ride to market. It was a very cold day, and the *aga* was shivering from head to toe.

"Are you freezing, boy?" he asked the young stable boy.

"No," answered the stable boy. "What about you, *aga*? Are you freezing?"

"I am. Why is it that you're almost naked, but you aren't freezing? I'm dressed warmly, yet I'm cold."

"Well, *aga*," the little stable boy explained, "when the cold goes into my jacket, it comes out here." He pointed to the holes in the elbows of his jacket.

"When the cold goes into your jacket, there are no holes through which it can escape. It has to stay inside. That's why you're cold."

In his simplicity, the boy reasoned so. In actuality, the boy was warm because he worked so hard, and the *aga* was cold because he let others work for him while he did nothing. ❂

Nasradin Hodja

(Yugoslavia—Kosovo and Metohija)

Note: Nasradin Hodja is a clever man, popular in the oral literature of Muslim tradition. There are many stories about him outwitting the wealthy and dishonest and defending the poor and pure of heart. One such story follows.

A merchant traveling on business came to an inn and spent the night there. For supper he dined on five boiled eggs.

In the morning, he left bright and early and forgot to pay the innkeeper for his supper. He remembered it only when he arrived home.

"Oh, for goodness sake, I forgot to pay for my supper!" he exclaimed. "If the inn were a little closer, I'd return to pay my debt today. Ah, well, when I chance to go that way again, I'll pay the innkeeper honorably, and I'll give him interest besides."

Many years later, he went to the same inn to spend the night. He summoned the innkeeper immediately in order to beg his pardon for forgetting to pay him and to give him the money he owed, with interest.

"Here you are, sir," he said. "Here's the price of the meal and the interest that I owe for those five eggs." He offered him a considerable sum of money.

"I won't accept it. It's not enough," the owner answered. "Five eggs over an extended period of time hatch into five hens.

"Each of those five hens would have laid ten eggs apiece. Ten eggs per hen make fifty eggs.

"Those fifty eggs would have hatched into fifty hens. They would have produced ten eggs apiece, too. That makes 500 eggs.

"Those 500 eggs would have became 500 hens. Ten eggs per 500 hens make 5,000 eggs, and that comes to much, much more than you have given me."

The merchant refused to listen to him, so the innkeeper brought charges against him. The judge ordered the merchant to pay the requested sum, and the merchant departed greatly upset.

On the road, he met Nasradin Hodja. When Nasradin Hodja saw the merchant's worried look, he asked him what was wrong.

"You can't help me," the merchant said. "What's the use of telling you? But I'll tell you anyway, in order to ease my troubled heart."

He told the whole story in detail, as if by repeating it he would be better able to understand it himself.

"That's not such a difficult problem," Nasradin Hodja said. "Go and request a hearing. Register me as your lawyer."

The merchant had nothing to lose, so he obeyed.

Some time passed and a policeman came to summon Nasradin Hodja to the courthouse.

"Tell the judge that I can't come now because I'm boiling rye for seed," Nasradin Hodja told the policeman.

The policeman scratched his head in perplexity, but he returned and relayed Nasradin Hodja's message to the judge.

At the second summons, Nasradin Hodja answered the same way, and only at the third summons did he go with the policeman to court.

"Where were you, and what were you doing?" the judge asked him.

"I told you that I was boiling rye for seed."

"Go on, you fool! How on earth can boiled grain sprout into plants?" the judge shouted at him.

"Why, in the same way that boiled eggs can hatch into chickens, your honor," Nasradin Hodja answered.

When he heard Nasradin Hodja's reply, the judge was ashamed of himself. He admitted that he had sentenced the merchant unjustly and told him to pay only for the five boiled eggs.

The happy merchant rewarded Nasradin Hodja richly and returned home. ❀

Honest Labor Is Always Rewarded

(Yugoslavia—Serbia)

Once upon a time there lived a very poor man. This poor man took a job working for a rich man without even coming to an agreement concerning wages. After working for a year, he went to his master for his pay.

His master gave him a single coin and said, "Take this for your service."

The poor man took the coin, thanked his master, and went in the direction of a swift stream. He arrived at the stream and thought, My goodness, my goodness, is it possible that I earned only one little coin for an entire year's labor? But who knows, perhaps I didn't deserve even that much. Let's put it to the test. I'll throw the coin into the water. If it doesn't sink, that means I got exactly as much as I deserved—one coin. If the coin does sink, then I didn't deserve even the coin I received."

The poor man made the sign of the cross and said, "Gracious Lord, if I deserve this coin, let it float. If not, let it sink."

He threw the coin into the water, and it immediately sank to the bottom. The poor man bent over, grabbed it, and took it back to his master.

"Here you are, master. Here is your coin. I still haven't earned it, so I'm staying on to serve you for another year."

At the end of the year, he went to his master again for his wages, to receive whatever his master would give him.

His master gave him a single coin again and said, "Take this for your service."

The poor man took the coin, thanked his master, and set out for the stream. Once again he made the sign of the cross and threw the coin into the water.

"Gracious Lord, if I deserve this coin, let it float. If not, let it sink."

Once again the coin went to the stream's bottom. The poor man retrieved it and took it to his master. "Here is your coin, master. I still haven't earned it, so I'll work for you a third year."

He worked the third year, then went to his master for his wages to receive whatever his master would give him. Once again, his master gave him a single coin.

The poor man accepted the coin, thanked his master, and went to the stream again. There, he made the sign of the cross and threw the coin into the water. "Gracious Lord, if I deserve this coin, let it float. If not, let it sink."

This time the coin did not sink; it floated. The poor man was happy. He plucked the coin out of the water and put it into his pocket. Then he went into the forest and built himself a small hut and began living in it.

Soon he learned that his former master was planning to sail the seas to another kingdom. He went to him and asked him to buy something there for him with the coin he had earned. The master promised he would, then set sail.

In one of the ports he traveled to, he met some children. They were carrying a cat with the intention of doing away with it by throwing it into the sea.

He went up to them and asked, "What are you doing?"

"He's a bad cat, and we want to be rid of him," the children explained.

The poor man's master took out the coin and offered it in exchange for the cat. The children agreed gladly and accepted the coin as payment for the animal.

The master took the cat on deck and sailed away. The ship sailed on and on under blue skies.

One day, a strong wind began blowing and carried the ship to heaven knows where. For three months it could not get back onto its proper course. Finally, the wind died down.

The master did not know where the ship had drifted. After sailing on for a short time, he put in at an unknown port.

Rumor had already spread that a ship from a foreign land was arriving, and the townspeople had gathered to look at it.

One of the local inhabitants, a rich man, came to the shore's edge and invited the ship's master to dine with him that evening.

"I accept your invitation gladly," the master said.

That evening, when he went to the rich man's house—oh, horror of horrors—rats and mice were running all around the room. The servants were attempting to drive them away with sticks.

The guest questioned his wealthy host. "Pardon me, brother, but what's going on here?"

"We've had to put up with this for centuries, brother. We can't dine or sup in peace. At night we have to sleep in a trunk so that the rats won't be able to gnaw off our ears."

The guest remembered the cat he had bought for a single coin and said to his host, "I have a beast on board ship who can exterminate all of the mice and rats within a period of two or three days."

"If you have such a beast, give him to us, brother. In exchange, I'll fill your ship full of gold and silver."

After dining, the guest went to his ship and brought back the cat. He told his host that it was not necessary to sleep in the trunk at night anymore. However, no one believed him and everyone, with the exception of the guest, crawled into their trunks again.

Honest Labor Is Always Rewarded

When it quieted down, the cat began catching mice and rats and piling them up into an enormous heap. But, many of the pests managed to run away and escape. In the morning, everyone saw the enormous pile of rats and mice in the middle of the room. The rats and mice that had managed to escape, thereby saving their skins, peeked out of their holes, but they dared not venture out of their sanctuary.

In three days all of the mice and rats were gone. The grateful host filled the traveler's ship with gold and silver, and the traveler returned to his homeland.

When he arrived, his former servant asked what he had bought with the coin. The master grabbed a piece of marble, beautifully trimmed, and gave it to the servant. "Take it. This is what I bought with your coin."

The servant was happy. He took the marble to his hut and made a sturdy table out of it.

In the morning, the poor man went to fetch wood. When he returned, the hut was glowing and the table was shining like the sun. The marble had turned to pure gold.

The servant took fright and ran to the master. "What on earth did you bring me? Come look! Is it really mine?"

The master went to the servant's hut and saw what wonder had occurred. "Well, what's to be done, son?" he asked. "Honest labor is always rewarded. Come collect your property."

He gave him all the gold and silver he had taken on board ship as reward at the town infested with mice and rats. And he gave the poor man his daughter's hand in marriage. The servant lived happily ever after and never knew poverty again. ✿

Two Coins

There once lived a poor man who traded whatever he could lay hands on to keep hunger away from his door. Nothing came of whatever trade he undertook. Finally, he understood that he was just unlucky and decided to find a simpleton he could trick.

He gathered some moss and put it in a sack. On top of the sack, he placed a bit of wool, and then he set out for market to sell his invention as a sack of wool.

On the way, he met a man who was going to market, too, carrying nut-galls with the intention of selling them in place of the real nuts with which they were covered.

The poor men struck up a conversation. "What are you carrying in your sack?" one asked.

"I've got nuts in my sack. What do you have?"

"I have wool in my sack."

"Let's exchange our wares. You take the nuts, and give me the wool. Then Mom can knit me some warm socks. I won't have to go about barefoot anymore."

"All right, why not! I've wanted a taste of nuts for some time now," the man with the moss declared. "But wool is more expensive than nuts, so if you want my wool you must pay an additional sum."

They began bargaining, and each tried to deceive the other. The man with the nuts did not want to pay an additional sum for the wool, but was agreeable to a trade. The man with the moss decided that in any event the nuts were more expensive than the moss he was carrying and that, nevertheless, he would stand to gain.

They bargained for a long time and finally decided that the man carrying the nuts should pay an additional two coins for the wool. However, he did not have two coins with him. He asked for payment to be postponed and said he would get the money when he went home. But the other man wanted to wait a while, for he knew that when the man returned home he would discover the deception. In order to have greater assurance that the debt would be paid, the two men became sworn brothers and declared eternal friendship.

Then, they exchanged sacks and went their separate ways, each with a sly grin, thinking that he had duped the other. When they arrived at their respective homes and took the wares they had exchanged out of their sacks, they found that they had deceived each other.

Time passed. The man who had sold moss, instead of wool, went to search for his sworn brother in order to get the two coins owed him. He found the debtor in a village working for the priest.

"Sworn brother," he said, "you deceived me."

"Well, you deceived me, too, brother," the other man answered.

The former man began demanding his two coins. "You must do what you agreed to do. Give me the two coins you owe me. Our bargain was sealed when we swore eternal brotherhood."

"I would give you the coins gladly, but I don't have two coins right now. However, you know, there is a big hole behind the house of the priest I work for. He climbs down into it quite often. It is probably filled with money and jewels. Come this evening and lower me into the hole. When we have cleaned it out and divided the loot, I'll pay you the two coins."

The other man agreed. That evening, when everyone was asleep, the priest's worker took a sack and a rope. He went to the hole with his sworn brother, climbed into the sack, and his brother lowered him into the hole on a rope.

Once in the hole, he got out of the sack and began feeling around, but he found nothing, except grain.

Then, he thought, If I tell my brother that there's nothing here, he'll leave and abandon me here in this hole. And the priest will scold me, too, if he ever finds me here.

He climbed back into the sack, tied it tightly with a rope, and cried out to his sworn brother, "Pull up the sack, brother. It's full of valuables."

His brother hauled the sack up and started thinking, Why should I divide anything with my brother? I'll take the whole sack, and he can just get himself out of the hole whatever way he can. The priest will pull him out in the morning.

He threw the sack with his sworn brother inside over his shoulder and ran to the village. A pack of barking dogs began chasing him.

He ran on. When he grew tired of running, the sack began to droop. Suddenly, he heard his brother's voice. "Pull the sack up, brother. The dogs are nipping at me."

Breathing heavily, the duped man hurled the sack onto the ground. The man sitting in the sack crawled out and declared, "So, you wanted to cheat me, brother!" "You cheated me, too," the other answered.

After a long argument, the debtor pledged to pay the two coins when his brother came the next time, whereupon they parted.

A long time passed. The priest's hired hand married and started a home of his own. One day he was sitting on the porch with his wife. He looked into the distance and saw his sworn brother heading in the direction of his home.

"Wife," he said, "my sworn brother is coming. I owe him two coins. I promised to give him them when he came. This is what we'll do. I'll go into the house and lie down. You put the covers over me and pretend you are grieving. Lament over me. If he thinks I have died, he'll return home without demanding that the debt be paid."

He went into his room, lay on his back, and crossed his arms on his chest. His wife covered him with a blanket and began lamenting and tearing out her hair. "Oh, dear husband, why have you left poor me all alone in this world?"

At that moment the sworn brother approached the house. "May God help you," he said. "Is this the home of my sworn brother?"

Through her tears the woman answered, "Yes, it is. Oh, woe is me, unhappy cuckoo that I am. My husband is lying here dead."

"May God give his soul peace! He was my sworn brother. We worked and traded together. Since such a misfortune has occurred, I will stay, of course, to accompany him to the grave and to throw a handful of earth onto his coffin."

The woman said, "The funeral is not going to be right away. You'll have to wait a long time, so you'd better just leave and be on your way."

"Heaven preserve us, how could I abandon my sworn brother? I'll wait, even if it takes three days, so that I can accompany him on his final journey."

The woman went into the house and told her husband quietly what had happened. He ordered her to fetch the priest and announce that he had died. "Let them take me to the chapel beside the cemetery. Then my brother will leave."

His wife told the priest, who came in the company of several men. The "deceased" was placed on a stretcher and carried to the chapel, where he was left overnight so that in the morning the burial service could be read and he could be buried.

Everyone left. Only the sworn brother announced that he would not for anything leave his brother, with whom he had traded and shared hospitality for so many years. He declared that he would stand guard beside him all night, and he remained in the chapel.

That night a band of robbers entered the village. They had robbed several wealthy homes and had stolen a great deal of money, clothing, and weapons.

While passing the chapel, one of them noticed that a candle was burning. "Let's go into the chapel and divide our loot," he suggested.

The sworn brother saw that armed men were entering the chapel, so he hid behind the altar. The robbers sat down and began dividing the money by placing an equal amount of coins in each robber's cap. Then, they divided the clothing and weapons haphazardly.

Everything went well, and they agreed on the division of their spoils until only one saber remained, which everyone wanted to receive. One of them grabbed it, jumped up, and said, "Let's try the blade out on that corpse to see if it is as good as it seems to be. If I can lop off his head with one blow, that means it's a fine saber."

The robber made for the coffin. The "corpse" jumped up and cried, "Oh, spirits, where are you?"

"We're over here, and we're ready to attack," his sworn brother answered from behind the altar.

When the robbers heard a voice speaking, they flung down the saber, left their piles of money, and ran away without so much as a backward glance.

They kept running until they were out of breath. When they came to a halt in the forest, their leader said, "Hey, brothers, we have wandered day and night through all kinds of forests and frightening places. We have fought with brave men and attacked forts and palaces. Not once did we tremble, and here we are afraid of a corpse. Is there perhaps a bold man among us who would return and see what's happening in the chapel?"

"I won't go," said one of them.

"I'm afraid," another declared.

"I'd rather attack ten living men than one dead man," said a third.

Finally, a robber was found who agreed to go back. He went to the cemetery beside the chapel. He crawled up to the chapel window quietly and began listening. In the chapel, the sworn brothers were dividing the robbers' money, clothing, and weapons peacefully.

Soon the conversation came round to the two coins. The "corpses" began quarreling and almost came to blows. The robber heard a shriek. "Where are my two coins? Give me my two coins!"

At that moment the debtor saw the robber beneath the window. He stuck his hand out quickly and grabbed the hat off the robber's head. He stretched the hat out to his sworn brother, and said, "You and your confounded two coins! Here's your two coins for you!"

The robber ran away in fright. He ran up to the others in the band, beside himself with terror, and said with his teeth chattering, "Well, brothers, it's lucky that we got away alive. There's an army of corpses in there. We divided the money up by the capful, but so great a number of corpses came to divide the money we left behind that each one received only two coins apiece. There weren't enough coins to go around, and the last corpse complained something terrible. Finally, one of the corpses took the cap off my head and gave it to the one who was complaining as his share."

The robbers, after listening to his tale, began running away from the so-called army of corpses. Both of the sworn brothers became wealthy, thanks to the robbers' loot. They lived quietly and peacefully and never tried to cheat anyone again. ✿

Glossary and Pronunciation Guide

Adriatic (aay-dree-AT-ic) **Sea**: located between Croatia, Montenegro, and Albania to the east and Italy to the west.

Afanasyev, Aleksandr (ah-fahn-AHS-yev, ah-lyek-SAHNDR): nineteenth-century collector of Russian folklore (1826–1871), responsible for compiling an eight-volume collection of Russian folktales (1855–1863).

aga (AH-gah): Muslim title of respect.

Albania (al-BAY-nee-ya): a country located on the Adriatic Sea. Its neighbors are Macedonia, Montenegro, Serbia, and Greece.

Albanian (al-BAY-nee-yan): an inhabitant of Albania; the language; of or pertaining to Albania.

Allah (AH-lah): the Muslim deity who, with the prophet Mohammed, forms the foundation of Islam.

Amazon (AM-ah-zawn): a female warrior in Greek mythology.

bajka (BYE-ka): fairy tale.

Belgrade (BEL-grayd): capital of Yugoslavia and Serbia.

Bey Zlatum (BAY, ZLAH-toom): *Bey* is a Turkish title indicating respect and high rank. *Zlatum* is an invented last name related to the word *zlato*, meaning "gold."

Bjelice (BYE-lee-tseh): an area in Montenegro.

Bosnia and Herzegovina (BAWZ-nee-ya, HER-tseh-go-VEE-nah): a former republic of Yugoslavia presently divided into the Federation of Bosnia and Herzegovina and the Serbian Republic, loosely held together by a central government.

Bosnian (BAWZ-nee-yan): an inhabitant of Bosnia; of or pertaining to Bosnia.

Bulgar (BOOL-gar): an inhabitant of Bulgaria; of or pertaining to Bulgaria. Historically the Bulgars formed the largest horde of the Hunnic state. Many of them settled in the Balkans and were assimilated into the Slavic population.

Ćele kula (CHEH-leh, KOO-lah): Skull Tower, a tower erected by the Turks to commemorate a military victory. It was composed of the skulls of defeated Serbs.

Communism (KAWM-yoo-nizm): a socialist form of government no longer as influential as it once was. Communism supports the interests of the state over those of the individual. It has a one-party system and a centralized economy. Yugoslavia, Russia, and other nations of the Soviet bloc were Communist.

Croatia (krow-AY-shah): former republic of Yugoslavia, now an independent country.

Croats (KROW-ats): people living in Croatia and surrounding areas.

Ćuprilić (choop-REEL-ich): last name of the Grand Vizier in the Montenegrin legend, "A Copper Coin or Your Head."

Cveta (SVET-ah): female first name.

Cyril (SIH-ril): ninth-century Greek missionary who created the Slavic alphabet.

Cyrillic (sih-RIL-ik): of or pertaining to the Slavic alphabet.

Dacia (DAY-shah): an ancient region, roughly corresponding to modern Romania, once inhabited by Thracians.

Dalmatia (dahl-MAY-shya): area on the coast of the Adriatic Sea, mostly in Croatia, but also in Montenegro.

dervish (DER-vish): a Muslim dedicated to a life of poverty and purity.

dinar (DEE-nahr): a monetary unit composed of one hundred *para*. A *para* is the smallest monetary unit.

Dubrovnik (doo-BROV-nik): Croatian port on the Adriatic Sea referred to as the "pearl of the Adriatic." The town is steeped in history and is known for its architectural masterpieces, literature, and great beauty.

Dukljan (DOO-klyahn): Tsar Dukljan's name is possibly related to the word *Duklja*, designating an area that belonged to the Romans and later the Byzantines. The Slavic tribes were united under this name.

Dušan, Stefan (DOO-shan, stef-AHN): emperor (1331–1355) during Serbia's golden age. After his death, large areas fell to the Ottoman Turks.

Ero (EH-roh): a popular trickster character in South Slavic folklore.

Fates (FAYTZ): in Greek and Roman mythology three old women who dispense each person's lot in life at birth.

Grimm (GRIM): name of brothers Jakob (1785–1863) and Wilhelm (1786–1859), collectors of German folktales. They figure importantly in the romantic movement and in the preservation of German folklore.

guslari (GOOS-lar-ee): folksingers who play the *gusle*.

gusle (GOOS-leh): a one-stringed Balkan musical instrument.

Hapsburg (HAPS-burg): the ruling house of Austria-Hungary, Spain, and the Roman Empire. Hapsburg rule extended from the thirteenth to the nineteenth century.

Illyria (ee-LEER-ee-ya): an ancient region located on the Adriatic Sea.

Illyrian (ee-LEER-ee-yan): an inhabitant of ancient Illyria; of or pertaining to Illyria.

Islam (IZ-lahm): the Muslim religion in which Allah is the deity worshiped, and Mohammed is the main prophet.

Istria (EES-tree-yah): a peninsula, located in northwest Croatia across from Italy, jutting out into the Adriatic Sea.

Janček (YAHN-chek): Slovenian male first name.

Karaždić, Vuk Stefanović (KAH-rahd-zich, VOOK, ste-FAHN-aw-vich): the most important Serbian writer (1784–1864) of his day. He was founder of the modern Serbian language and collector and recorder of Serbian folklore.

kolo (KOH-loh): a traditional round dance performed in a circle.

Kosovo and Metohija (KAW-soh-voh, meh-TOKH-ee-yah): southern section of Yugoslavia, recently ravaged by civil war.

Kosovo (KAW-soh-voh) **Field**: site of the famous battle in which the Turks defeated the Serbs in 1389, thereby bringing 500 years of occupation and cultural darkness to the Balkans.

Koštunica, Vojislav (KAW-shtun-ee-tsah, VOY-ee-slahv): elected president of Yugoslavia in September, 2000.

Kuškundaljevo (KUSH-koon-DAHL-yev-aw): an invented fairy-tale village.

lasta (LAHS-tah): South Slavic word for "swallow."

Ljubljana (LYOOB-lyah-nah): the capital of Slovenia.

Macedonia (mass-eh-DOH-nee-ya): an independent country, once a republic of the former Yugoslavia, located north of Greece.

Macedonian (mass-eh-DOH-nee-yan): an inhabitant of Macedonia; the language; of or pertaining to Macedonia.

Mecca (MEHK-ah): holy city of the Muslims and birthplace of Mohammed, their prophet.

Methodius (meth-OH-dee-us): Greek missionary to the Slavs who, with his brother Cyril, devised the Glagolitic alphabet, ancestor to the Cyrillic alphabet.

Milošević, Slobodan (mee-LOH-sheh-vich, SLOH-bah-dan): past president of the Federal Republic of Yugoslavia.

Montenegrin (mawn-tee-NEG-rin): an inhabitant of Montenegro; of or pertaining to Montenegro.

Montenegro (mawn-tee-NEG-roh): the only former republic of Yugoslavia, besides Serbia, that has remained a part of Yugoslavia.

mosque (MAWSK): a Muslim place of worship.

Mostar (MOH-stahr): ancient town in the southwestern corner of Bosnia and Herzegovina on the Neretva River.

Mrvaljević, Vukota (MRVAHL-ye-vich, VOO-kaw-tah): the Montenegrin *vojvoda*, or governor, who braved Turkish wrath and resisted paying a tax.

narodna proza (NAH-rohd-nah, PROH-zah): folk prose.

narodne pjesme (NAH-rohd-nye, PYES-mye): folk songs.

Nasradin Hodja (NAHS-rah-deen, HOH-dzah): A "hodja" is a Muslim priest. Nasradin Hodja is known for his wisdom in solving disputes and problems.

Nasreddin Afandi, also Efendi (NAHS-reh-deen, ah-FAHN-dee, ef-EHN-dee): hero of the Tadzhik satirical folk genre called the *latifa*. Like the Balkan Nasradin Hodja, he challenges the powerful and defends the oppressed with his quick wit.

nečiste sile (neh-CHEE-steh, SEE-leh): evil spirits, an expression used in reference to mischievous or wicked minor deities.

Niš (NEESH): a Serbian town located on the main road running southeast of Belgrade.

Njegoš, Petar Petrović (NYE-gosh, PEH-tahr peh-TROH-vich): Njegoš (Peter I) founded Montenegro as an independent state in 1799. The Njegoš family ruled until Nicholas I (1860-1918) was dethroned.

para (PAH-rah): a monetary unit comparable to our penny. There are 100 *para* in a *dinar*.

pasha (PAH-shah): a Turkish civil or military official.

Podgorica (PAWD-GORE-ee-tsah): the capital of Montenegro. It was called Titograd during the Communist era.

Psyche (SIGH-key): heroine of a Greek myth. As the bride of Eros, she had to undergo many difficulties to be reunited with her husband.

Rizvanbegović, Ali-Pasha (reez-vahn-BEG-aw-vich, AH-lee-PAH-shah): a Turkish official with the last name of Rizvanbegović.

Sarajevo (SAH-ra-yeh-voh): the capital of Bosnia and Herzegovina.

Serb (SURB): an inhabitant of Serbia and surrounding countries.

Serbia (SUR-bee-yah): the only republic, along with Montenegro, that remains a part of Yugoslavia.

Serbian (SUR-bee-yan): the language spoken by the Serbs; of or pertaining to Serbia.

Skopje (SKAWP-yeh): the capital of Macedonia.

Škrat (SHKRAT): Croatian name of folk character reminiscent of Rumplestiltskin.

Slavs (SLAHVZ): a group of people including the Southern Slavs (Serbs, Croats, Bulgars, Slovenians, Montenegrins, Macedonians, and Bosnians), the Eastern Slavs (Russians, Ukrainians, and Belorussians), and the Western Slavs (Poles, Czechs, and Slovaks).

Slovenia (sloh-VEE-nee-yah): a former republic of Yugoslavia; now an independent country.

Slovenian (sloh-VEE-nee-yahn): an inhabitant of Slovenia; the language spoken in Slovenia; of or pertaining to Slovenia.

Stari most (STAH-ree, MOHST): Old Bridge, after which the town of Mostar was named. It was designed in 1566 by the Turkish architect Hajrudin and destroyed in 1993 as a result of ethnic warfare. It stood as a symbol of a multi-ethnic Bosnia-Herzegovina.

Tadzhikistan, also Tajikistan (tah-DZEEK-is-tahn): country in Central Asia located north of Afghanistan. It was once part of the Soviet Union.

Tito (TEE-toh): Communist dictator of Yugoslavia from 1945–1980.

Thrace (THRAAYS): an ancient region formerly located on the east side of the Balkan Peninsula. It is not to be confused with the modern region located between Greece and Turkey.

Thracian (THRAAY-shen): an inhabitant of Thrace; of or pertaining to Thrace.

tsar (TSAHR): Slavic title of emperor.

tsarevich (TSAHR-ye-vich): son of a tsar.

tsarevna (TSAHR-yev-nah): daughter of a tsar.

tsaritsa (tsahr-EET-sah): wife of a tsar.

vila (VEE-lah): a minor deity. The vila usually lives in watery places found in the forests or mountains. She is comparable to a nymph or oread.

vizier (vee-ZEER): a high officer in the government of the Turkish Ottoman Empire.

vojvoda (VOY-vaw-dah): a governor or commander-in-chief.

Vojvodina (VOY-vaw-dee-nah): an autonomous region in Yugoslavia.

Yugoslavia (yoo-go-SLAHV-ee-yah): first established as a country in 1918 by a unified group of South Slavs. Later it became a Communist country ruled by Marshal Tito. Today it is composed of Serbia, including Vojvodina and Kosovo and Metohija, and Montenegro.

Zagreb (ZAH-greb): capital of Croatia and one of the centers of South Slavic culture.

Sources

Collections are in alphabetical order. Stories are listed in the order of their appearance in the text.

Bošković-Stulli, Maja, ed. *Istarske narodne priče*. Narodno stvaralaštvo istre, ed. Zoran Palčok, no. 1. Zagreb: Institut za narodnu umjetnost, 1959.

> "The Short Tail" (*Kratak rep*), 117.

Bovan, Vladimir, ed. *Srpske narodna pripovetke sa Kosova i Metohije*. Biblioteka Jedinstvo, ed. Pera Stefanović, no. 77. Priština: Jedinstvo, 1976.

> "The Mouse and the Ant" (*Miš i mravka*), 33.

> "The Aga and the Stable Boy" (*Aga i seiz*), 170.

> "Nasradin Hodja" (*Nasradin odža*), 167–68.

Brenkova, Kristina, ed. and comp. *Slovenske ljudske pripovedi*. Ljubljana: Mladinske Knjiga, 1970.

> "Nasta and the Sun" (*Pripovedka o soncu in Nasti*), 201–2.

> "The Little Hedgehog" (*Ježek*), 125–26.

Karadžić, Vuk Stefanović. *Srpske narodna pripovijetke*. In *Dela Vuka Karadžića*. Vol. 7. Miroslav Pantić, ed. Belgrade: Prosveta, 1969.

> "Tsar Dukljan" (*Car Dukljan*), 191–92.

> "The Bear, the Pig, and the Fox" (*Medved, svinja i lisica*), 215–16.

> "The Snake Bridegroom" (*Zmija mladoženja*), 101–03.

> "The Devil and His Apprentice" (*Đavo i njegov segrt*), 87–89.

> "The Magic Dagger" (*Čudotvorni nož),* 163–64.

> "You Reap What You Sow" (*Kako su radile onako su i prošle*), 161–62.

> "Ero and the Turk" (*Ero i Turčin*), 27.

Kotevska, Cveta, ed. *Biberče i druge narodna bajke*. Belgrade: Narodna knjiga, 1960.

"Baldy" (*Ćela*), 164–66.

Larits, L., comp. *Slavianskie narodnye skazki*. Uzhgorod: Zakarpatskoe oblastnoe izdatel'stvo, 1959.

"Three Eels" (*Tri ugria*), 84–86.

"Honest Labor Is Always Rewarded" (*Chestnyi trud ne propadaet darom*), 130–32.

"Two Coins" (*Dva grosha*), 153–57.

Prodanović, Jaša M., ed. *Antologija narodnih pripovedaka i ostalih proznih umotvorina*. Belgrade: Kultura, 1951.

"Škrat, the Wood Goblin" (*Škrat*), 207–9.

"The Twelve Crumbs" (*Dvanaest mrva*), 176–80.

Šijaković, Miodrag B. *Bajke jugoslovenskih naroda*. Glasovi naroda, ed. Berislav M. Nikolić, no. 6. Belgrade: Branko Bonović, 1964.

"The Little Shepherd" (*Pastriče*), 134–35.

"The Nightingale Empress" (*Bulbul-džizar*), 162–71.

"The Water Sprite" (*Vodenjak*), 142–45.

"The Young Man and His Vampire Brother" (*Mladić i njegov pobratim vampir*), 173–75.

"The Shepherd and the Three Vilas" (*Ovčar i tri vile*), 103–09.

Zuković, Ljubomir, comp. *Narodna proza: priče, bajke, basne, pitalice, zagonetke i po-slovice*. Biblioteka lektira, ed. Rajko Nogo. Sarajevo: Veselin maleša, 1973.

"Why Man Lives Eighty Years" (*Otkuda čovjeku osamdeset godina*), 193–94.

"The Miser and the Generous Man" (*Tivtiz i džomet*), 110–13.

"A Copper Coin or Your Head" (*Metelik ili glavu*), 257.

"Beautiful Mara" (*Lepa Mara*), 76–79.

"The Ox and the Mouse" (*Voi i miš*), 204.

"The Horse and the Wolf" (*Konj i vuk*), 199–200.

"Bey Zlatum" (*Zlatumbeg*), 132–37.

"How the Order Was Obeyed" (*Kako vrši naredbu*), 246.

"It's Not Easy to Steal From a Gypsy" (*Ciganinu nije lasno ukrasti*), 254.

Index

159

About the Author

Author, teacher, translator, and folklorist, Bonnie C. Marshall is Adjunct Instructor and Curriculum Coordinator for the Russian Program at Johnson C. Smith University, where she teaches Russian. A native of New Hampshire, she received her education from Boston University, Assumption College, and the University of North Carolina, as well as from three institutions of higher learning in Russia (Moscow State University, Leningrad State University, and the Herzen Institute). Dr. Marshall studied folklore under Charles G. Zug and Vasa D. Mihailovich at the University of North Carolina and under professors Alla Vasilievna Kulagina and Vladimir Prokopievich Anikin at Moscow State University. Her collection of Russian folklore *Baba Yaga's Geese and Other Russian Stories* won the Chicago Book Clinic Award, and her picture book *Grasshopper to the Rescue* was a Junior Literary Guild Selection. She has done fieldwork in Russia collecting songs, *chastushki* (four-line folk lyrics), and anecdotes. She resides in Meredith, New Hampshire.

About the Editor

Vasa D. Mihailovich, Professor Emeritus of Slavic Languages and Literature at the University of North Carolina, Chapel Hill, was born in 1926 in Yugoslavia and immigrated to the United States in 1951, where he received his Ph.D. with the thesis "Hermann Hesse and Russia." He has published, in Serbo–Croatian, six books of prose poems and two books of short stories. He has also edited or co-edited anthologies, *Introduction to Yugoslav Literature* (1973), *White Stones and Fir Trees: An Anthology of Slavic Literature* (1977), *Contemporary Yugoslav Poetry* (1977), *Serbian Poetry from the Beginnings to the Present* (1988), *Songs of the Serbian People: From the Collections of Vuk St. Karadžić* (1997), as well as books of literary criticism and literary history, *Modern Slavic Literature* (1972, 1976), *Dictionary of Literary Biography: South Slavic Writers Before World War II* (1994), and *South Slavic Writers Since World War II* (1997). He has compiled several volumes of the bibliography of Yugoslav and Russian writers and translated, among other works, the greatest Serbian epic, *Gorski vijenac—The Mountain Wreath* by Petar Petrović Njegoš. A member of the Association of Serbian Writers in Belgrade, he is on the editorial board of *World Literature Today*.